'Joy Rees has the gift of explaining theoretical concepts in a straightforward and jargon-free manner and of empowering adults – whether social workers, adopters or foster carers – to feel confident in tackling what is a complex and sensitive task. Joy's book is a practical guide and includes a wealth of examples of ways to frame sad and difficult stories without leaving the child feeling responsible.'

– Jeanne Kaniuk OBE, Managing Director, Coram Adoption

'This book has been my go-to guide in terms of constructing family friendly life stories since its publication – I'm thrilled to see that this 2nd edition broadens the scope to include children in foster care or special guardianship arrangements, as well as adoption, as Rees' model fits them perfectly. Busy practitioners will love the selection of sensitively written sample stories that will prove invaluable in ensuring all children who need them have timely access to a child friendly life story book – a book that their adopters and carers will use with confidence to support their children to integrate their histories.'

– Katie Wrench, author of Helping Vulnerable Children and Adolescents to Stay Safe: Building Protective Behaviours

T0271455

LIFE STORY BOOKS
FOR ADOPTED AND FOSTERED CHILDREN

A FAMILY FRIENDLY APPROACH

second edition

Joy Rees

Foreword by Alan Burnell
Illustrated by Jamie Goldberg

Jessica Kingsley *Publishers*
London and Philadelphia

First edition published in 2009
This second edition published in 2017
by Jessica Kingsley Publishers
73 Collier Street
London N1 9BE, UK
and
400 Market Street, Suite 400
Philadelphia, PA 19106, USA

www.jkp.com

Library of Congress Cataloging in Publication Data
Rees, Joy.
  Life story books for adopted children : a family friendly approach / Joy
Rees ; foreword by Alan Burnell ; illustrated by Jamie Goldberg.
       p. cm.
  Includes bibliographical references (p.   ) and index.
  ISBN 978-1-84310-953-2 (pb : alk. paper) 1. Adopted children-
-Family relationships. 2. Diaries (Blank-books) I. Title.
  HV875.R36 2009
  362.734--dc22
                                   2008040884

British Library Cataloguing in Publication Data
A CIP catalogue record for this book is available from the British Library

ISBN 978 1 78592 167 4
eISBN 978 1 78450 436 6

Printed and bound in Great Britain

Download your resources

Sample life story books can be downloaded at www.jkp.com/voucher using
the code REESLIFESTORY for personal use with this program, but may not
be reproduced for any other purposes without the permission of the publisher.

In memory of my mother, Margaret,
affectionately known
by family and friends as

'Peggy Groesffordd'

1918–2015

At 97 years old, and with advanced dementia,
she remained loving and playful and continued
to remind me of the importance of family and
of the need to be claimed and to belong.

Contents

Foreword

This brave little book addresses one of the more complex issues in social work today. Preparing life story books for children became part of social work practice in the 1970s. At that time, they were designed to give young adopted children a sense of continuity and identity. There was research evidence at the time that suggested that, because of the closed nature of adoption, young people and adults who had been adopted as babies suffered from 'genealogical bewilderment'.

However, the population of children who are placed for adoption today invariably have experienced adverse and traumatic environments in infancy. We now realize that such children suffer developmental trauma as a consequence. Joy Rees' book is designed to help social workers construct life story books that acknowledge those early difficult experiences in an honest and open way. Joy's advice on how to do this is based on her understanding of how early trauma affects children's memory and their ability to regulate themselves, hence her recommendation that parents should be involved in the process. We have learned from attachment theory that children who are adopted need to develop 'a coherent narrative' and Joy's book endeavours to provide a format in which social workers can help children and parents do this together.

I recommend this book to social workers who have the complex task of compiling life story books for adopted children. The simplicity of its approach belies the sophistication of the thinking and theory that lies behind it.

Alan Burnell, Co-Director of Family Futures
2016

Acknowledgements

Many thanks to my husband Gwyn, my children, Sian and Owen, my sister Janet and my favourite (and one and only) niece, Joanna. Their enthusiasm, support and advice have been invaluable.

Much gratitude also goes to my ex-colleagues in the Adoption Support Team at Surrey for their encouragement when I began writing life story books in a 'back to front' way, some 16 years ago. Also to Alan Burnell at Family Futures, who read the first draft of this book, saw the potential and suggested publication.

A big thank you to Jamie for his illustrations.

Last, but certainly not least, I am indebted to the many adopted adults, especially the amazing Jane, who has helped so many others find 'the missing pieces of their jigsaws', and to the adoptive parents and wonderful children and young people I have enjoyed meeting over the years. They have been truly inspirational!

Introduction

Compiling life story books for adopted children has been part of good social work practice for the last 40 years, though early life books were little more than scrap books or photograph albums. Recent versions tend to give a more coherent narrative, and, using a selection of photographs, drawings, diagrams and documents, provide a very detailed account of a child's life journey.

This good practice was endorsed by the Adoption and Children Act 2002, and the provision of life story books has been firmly embedded in adoption statutory guidance and standards since, although, as highlighted in the research conducted by the children's charity, Coram, and Bristol University, 'there was a broad consensus [amongst adopters] that many books were of poor quality...and agencies did not seem to prioritize life story books' (Coram/Bristol University 2015, p.2).

Furthermore, although there is an expectation that some direct work should be undertaken with all children to help them understand why they came into care, the practice of compiling life story books has not been extended to include those who are not adopted, but who will need alternative substitute care and support throughout childhood and beyond.

Other routes to permanency include long-term foster carers, kinship carers (i.e. family, friend or other connected person) and those living with Special Guardians. Many of these children have particularly complex histories, confusing family dynamics and may have experienced multiple moves. As with adopted children, they also need help in piecing together their early histories and fragmented life journeys.

In essence, therefore, life story books should provide answers to the many questions all these children are likely to have – but may be reluctant to ask – about their early life experiences: the 'what happened', 'when' and 'why' questions.

A life story book is basically, as Vera Fahlberg (2003) says, 'a chronology of the child's life, helping the young person to understand and remember what has happened to him or her in the past' (p.354).

Having a clear understanding of his or her own history is seen as 'grounding' and of paramount importance as this enables the child to live more comfortably in the present and to plan for the future.

It is now generally agreed that the main aims of a life story book are:

- to give details and understanding of the child's history

- to build the child's sense of identity

- to enable the child to share their past with their adopters, carers and others

- to give a realistic account of early events and to dispel fantasies about the birth family

- to link the past to the present and to help both the child and the adopter/carer to understand how earlier life events continue to impact on behaviour

- to acknowledge issues of separation and loss

- to enable adoptive parents and carers to understand and develop empathy for the child

- to enhance the child's self-esteem and self-worth

- to promote attunement and attachment

- to help the child to develop a sense of security and permanency.

Traditionally, to achieve these aims, life story books have started with the child's past – often unintentionally but inevitably feeding directly into the trauma and into the child's sense of shame and blame. This could be avoided by starting with the present and with life in the permanent placement.

My approach allows the child to explore past trauma from the safety of a secure base. By turning the list of aims 'on its head' and concentrating on the last three, the rest should follow and the child's sense of self and understanding of their history can develop over time and evolve at the child's pace.

CHAPTER 1

A New Approach

The traditional approach: Past → Present

As noted, life story books are generally only produced for children who are adopted and as such they are considered to be the essential 'tool' that an adoptive parent can use to help their child gain a sense of identity and an understanding of their history. To achieve this, the book usually starts with the child's birth and details of the birth family, and progresses chronologically to the present, ending with the adoption. As Beth O'Malley (2004) stresses, 'A lifebook starts with the child's birth, not their arrival into their adoptive family' (p.8). Adoptive parents tend to be relegated to the end of the book and in some instances they only appear on the very last page.

This traditional structure often proves uncomfortable for both adoptive parent and child. It may be too direct, threatening, painful and confusing, and as a consequence the book is often put away or damaged. This suggests that a different approach to the construction of life story books is needed.

By changing the format the book can be used primarily to encourage secure family attachments and a sense of permanency, and ultimately this may be far more effective in helping children to acquire a more positive and integrated sense of identity and a greater understanding of their history. We need to achieve this for all children in permanent care, not only for those who are adopted.

A new approach:
Present → Past → Present → Future

'Our sense of self is closely dependent on the few intimate attachment relationships we have or have had in our lives, especially our relationship with the person who raised us' (Bowlby 2007, p.viii). Furthermore, a child's sense of history and identity needs time to 'evolve'. This will happen in a less threatening and more positive way if life story books concentrate on facilitating healthy attachments and on giving the children a sense of belonging, of being claimed and of permanency and security.

To achieve this, the book should start not with the child's past but with the present; and end not with the present, but with a hopeful and encouraging future.

Designing the book so that the child's history is in the middle is symbolically significant. The history is not only shared openly, it is literally contained and embraced by their carers or adopters, so it may feel safer and more manageable for the child.

The past should not overwhelm the child and the history should be kept honest but short – in perspective in terms of the child's whole life. They have a long future ahead!

CHAPTER 2

A Life Story Book is Not...

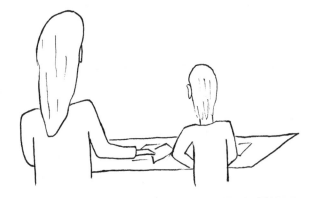

Life story work

There is sometimes confusion between life story work and a life story book. Life story work is generally considered to be the process of helping a child to understand his or her history, while the book is regarded as the end product. Using a variety of approaches – listening, talking, drawing, painting, playing, storytelling, compiling ecomaps, family trees or other diagrams, or using sand trays, puppets and interactive packages – life story work aims to help children to remember their life journey and unravel their confusions and misunderstandings about their past. 'Life story work is an attempt to give back some of this past to children separated from their families of origin' (Ryan and Walker 2016, p.4). It is about processing and internalizing the information. It is also seen as 'a therapeutic tool that deals with the child's inner world and how that relates to the child's perception of external reality' (Rose and Philpot 2005, p.15). Wrench and Naylor agree that 'the process of working through a child's story alongside him can be therapeutic in itself' (2013, p.10).

Fundamentally, life story work always involves the child, while the child is not always directly involved in writing the book. Indeed, Rose and Philpot (2005) acknowledge that although there are many ways of involving the child, the responsibility for writing the book is on the worker, and they also see the book as the end product and 'first and foremost, a clear account of what happened during the process of internalisation' (p.119). Certainly many elements of the life work can then be incorporated into the book. However, including too much of the actual work could confuse and distract from the child's understanding of their own story.

For older children placed with permanent carers there will be the opportunity to engage them in life story work, and the life story book can evolve from this. But many children placed with adoptive parents are too young or just too anxious to participate in any direct work, and they may need the book first to allay some of their fears. The book gives the child the basic narrative, and it can then be used by professionals or by carers and adoptive parents as the basis for future life story work. Sometimes the product needs to come first and the process of internalization follows.

Some other things a life story book is not:

- **A background history or a summary of the child's permanence report:** These reports are prepared for the Fostering or Adoption and Permanency Panels and other professional meetings. They give a very detailed account of the child's history. The carer or adoptive parents should have copies of these and will be able to share the content with the child, when they feel it would be helpful. After the age of 18 years, the child can also apply to the agency for access to this information.

- **A later life letter:** This is again a requirement in relation to adopted children. The letter is addressed to the child and written by the child's social worker. It is given to the adoptive parents for safekeeping. The letter contains more information and factual details to be shared with the child at a later stage – usually during the teenage years or earlier if appropriate. For young people in care, using the guidance and a similar format to the later life letter would be an effective way of providing them with a background summary.

- **A chronology:** This is a list of significant people, events, changes and movements since birth/pre-birth, with dates and ages. A chronology may also be produced in the form of a life graph or flow chart.

- **A photograph album:** Whilst every effort should be made to gather photographs of birth parents, siblings, other birth relatives, ex-foster carers and significant people in the child's life, with names, relationships and dates, they do not all need to be in the life story book. They should be kept in a separate album with a few scanned into the book.

- **A foster carers' memory book or box:** A memory book is usually a folder or ring binder with information, anecdotes, developmental milestones, photographs, cards, certificates and other mementos gathered while the child lived with the foster family. It is an extremely helpful way of preserving those precious early memories. Many foster carers are now also gathering other memorabilia – a favourite toy, item of clothing or other possessions, a lock of hair, those first milk teeth, copies of school reports, certificates, prizes and any other special trinkets or little souvenirs the child has gathered – and storing them in a customized box.

Foster carers' memory books and boxes contain extremely important 'treasures'. For children who have experienced many moves, their histories will have become fragmented and their memories, including happy memories, are so easily lost, so foster carers play a vital role in safeguarding these for the children in their care.

All of the above are important and should be given to the permanent carer or adoptive parents, with explanations. They can all be shared with the child when appropriate. However, none of them are substitutes for the life story book.

CHAPTER 3

A Different Perspective

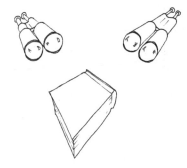

With greater understanding of attachments and of the impact of early relationships and early experiences on child development, including neurological development, it is clear that not only the format but also the focus of the life story book needs to change.

A life story book should be written in a way that reinforces a sense of permanency and stability, raises self-esteem, and promotes attunement and a secure attachment. Attachment is considered to be the bond that grows between a child and parent, while attunement is a parent's ability to understand their child's cries, sounds and facial expressions and to respond appropriately – it is the ability to see into their child's mind. Attunement is the base on which healthy, secure attachments are formed.

John Bowlby is considered to be the father of attachment theory. He maintained that human infants experience the world and their sense of self through their relationships with primary carers. All of us, from the cradle to the grave, are happiest when life is organized as 'a series of ever-lengthening excursions' from the secure base provided by those carers (Bowlby 2007, p.129). If the parent is stable and reliable, a source of safety, security and comfort, then a positive attachment will form and the child will develop a positive sense of self – and their world will be experienced as a safe place and one to be explored and enjoyed. The provision of this secure base is 'a central feature of [Bowlby's] concept of parenting' (Bowlby 1992, p.11).

Newborn babies are unable to survive alone. Their bodies and their brains are underdeveloped and they are completely dependent on a responsible adult to meet their physical and emotional needs. It is the quality of this first adult relationship that directly affects a child's psychological growth and development, and leads to secure or insecure attachment patterns.

To build a secure and strong attachment, certain types of interactions are essential and have often been referred to as the 'dance' or 'steps' of attachment (van Gulden and Riedel 1998–1999).

There are three very important stages of forming a secure attachment:

- **The interactive cycle of relaxation and arousal:** If a parent consistently recognizes and responds appropriately to the baby's state and satisfies their needs, a strong foundation of trust and security is laid down.

- **The falling in love stage:** The positive interactions between the child and parents, gazing into each other's eyes, cooing, smiling and generally respecting, valuing and enjoying each other's company.

- **The belonging and claiming process:** van Gulden stresses that, 'All humans need to feel that they belong in their families and that their family unit claims them' (van Gulden and Riedel 1998–1999, pp.3–9).

To be an effective tool for carers or adoptive parents, the steps of this dance need to be reflected in the life story book, and carers or adoptive parents clearly need a much higher profile. They must be allowed to claim their children and we must enable children to feel that they belong and are a valued member of the family.

CHAPTER 4

The Inner Child and Subliminal Messages

To understand the 'inner child' or the 'inner working model', we need to fully appreciate the significance of early relationships and experiences and recognize the impact that these have on a child's growth and development, and we also need to look in more detail at the different types of attachment. With this knowledge, we can raise a child's self-esteem and increase their self-worth by ensuring that appropriate, positive subliminal messages are incorporated throughout the life story book.

All children separated from their family of birth, for whatever reason, have experienced a loss. Verrier (2009) refers to the trauma of this separation as 'the primal wound'. Those who have also suffered neglect and abuse in their formative years are further traumatized and are often more confused about their past. Such children tend to hold themselves responsible for any ill-treatment they have suffered, have low self-esteem and a deep sense of shame. Many find it difficult to trust adults or to form secure attachments.

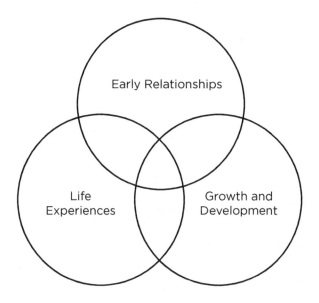

Bowlby (1992) identified the correlation between these three 'spheres' and how this affects the way children feel about themselves and how they see the world. The three spheres combine to shape a child's inner world. It is this 'inner working model', the child's core, which provides the key to understanding the child's current behaviour. In effect, a child's behaviour will tell you much about their history, and their history will explain their behaviour.

Early relationships

The quality of the first relationship is of prime importance. As this relationship begins to develop pre-birth, the first attachment is with the mother. The level and type of any parent-child attachment depends on the parent's emotional and physical availability, and on their ability to respond appropriately to the child's needs. If parents are attuned, they read their baby's signals and are able to meet his or her needs. Over time, a secure attachment is formed. Conversely, if a baby's needs are not met, an insecure attachment will form. This could be an 'avoidant', 'ambivalent' or 'disorganized' attachment, and some children at the extreme end of this continuum may be described as having 'disordered' attachment.

- **Avoidant:** When a parent is consistently unresponsive and unavailable to a child, and repeatedly ignores or rejects, the child eventually switches off. He or she becomes emotionally closed down, disassociates, feels unloved and avoids intimate relationships. There is no attunement or connection.

  These children adapt to this form of parenting by developing an emotional distance. They do not trust adults, so they become self-reliant and are often described as 'putting up a brick wall'. They need to maintain their independence, are reluctant to seek assistance and are seen as the controlling, bossy children. They may have difficulty making friends because of their intimacy issues and they fall out with those they have because of the need to be in charge.

- **Ambivalent:** If the quality of the parenting is inconsistent – one moment loving and affectionate and the next angry or agitated – the child becomes anxious and bewildered. The resulting 'mental models' are ones of unpredictability and insecurity. Having received such mixed messages from the parent, the world is now a very confusing place and life becomes an emotional roller coaster as these children experience the 'biological paradox': the adult that they need to go to for comfort and care is also the source of their anxiety.

  Despite such inconsistent parenting, these children often appear to be very attached to the parent. They are very dependent and 'clingy' as they try to remain physically close. They are reluctant to let the parent out of their sight in case they disappear. Such behaviour is often seen as a measure of 'good' attachment. In fact these children are constantly checking and are unsure when they will get their next meal, drink, cuddle, etc. They don't want to miss their chance, so they stay close. They are scared and anxious and as they get older they become the children who try to parent their parents. These children often remain within the family longer than is good for them as the damaging nature of their attachment is not always recognized. They are, in fact, in an emotionally lonely and fearful place and certainly deserve better parenting.

- **Disorganized:** This is the most worrying group. Children with avoidant or ambivalent attachment styles have developed some coping strategies. This third group of children is so confused that they have no effective strategies! Not only are their basic needs unmet, but they also experience their parents as very unpredictable, frightening figures. The parents' behaviour is often overwhelming and at times absolutely terrifying. These children experience an extreme version of the 'biological paradox'. This poses a great dilemma for them and they see no solution. Unable to make sense of this situation they mirror their parents' behaviour and they, too, become chaotic and disorganized. Life is exhausting for them as they must remain hypervigilant at all times.

  Children at the extreme end of this attachment spectrum are more vulnerable to mental health issues, especially during their teenage years. Some display behaviour associated with reactive attachment disorder (RAD), such as an aversion to touch or physical affection, a need to be in control and problems with anger management.

Children in the three groups have some common characteristics. They have negative inner working models and blame themselves for the poor parenting they have received. Most tend to feel unlovable, have low self-esteem and an innate sense of 'badness' and shame. They feel that their early negative experiences are their fault and they do not deserve better.

Life experiences

As discussed, a baby who experiences poor, neglectful parenting will develop an insecure attachment. Inconsistent or abusive parents cause further trauma. Children of such parents learn that they cannot trust adults to care for them, and their experiences make them more vulnerable and more susceptible to stress.

Attuned, attentive parents are able to soothe their children when they are distressed and help them to regulate their emotions. A child who is not helped to develop this ability will be driven by their emotions and will have poor impulse control. For these children, the world is a confusing and frightening place and they continually live on the verge of a fight, flight or freeze response. They become sensitized to stress, and are regarded as unpredictable as they appear to overreact to particular incidents or to unknown triggers.

In such a state, a child's general development is impaired, cognitive processes are impeded and thinking logically is just not possible. This further compounds their reputation of being 'unpredictable' children.

Growth and development

So a child's ability to grow and progress through the usual stages of development will be seriously impeded if they experience neglectful or abusive parenting. A secure attachment will not be established and further abuse will increase the trauma. This leads to additional stress. Without a responsive, soothing parent, emotions cannot be regulated, so the stress escalates.

Stress and anxiety use up enormous amounts of energy. This energy has to be diverted from other areas, leading to a reduced capacity for physical growth, neurological development and learning. This is evident in the child's behaviour as they struggle with common cognitive concepts that normally develop in the first few months or years of life, such as object constancy – infants gradually learn that objects, including people, have not disappeared if they cannot be touched or they are out of sight or earshot.

Such children may also have difficulty with cause and effect thinking, or be unable to grasp the concept of consequences or to see the world from other people's perspectives. This lack of flexibility of thought means that they find it hard to empathize. They therefore struggle with relationships, so have difficulty making or maintaining friends.

The inner working model

All children not able to stay with their birth parents have experienced a primal separation and loss, and they will have some attachment issues. Those who have been neglected or abused will have suffered further developmental trauma and have difficulties resulting from their insecure attachments, and will have a very negative 'inner working model'.

Children with a negative 'inner working model' will have a low sense of self-worth, a mistrust of adults and a perception of the world as an unsafe place. They are likely to lack inner confidence and may feel worthless and unloveable. Many of these children develop an inner sense of 'shame' or 'badness', blame themselves for their early experiences, and are 'primed' to expect further abuse or neglect. These misconceptions have been 'hard wired' into their brain – laid down in their unconscious memory – and attempting to access or change these inner beliefs at a conscious level will have little effect. Just telling children they are loveable and valued will not work. They need to feel this from the inside.

The importance of subliminal messages

Because the negative inner beliefs are laid down in the child's unconscious memory, they need to be addressed on an unconscious level. With this in mind, when writing a life story book, the child's history needs to be presented in a sensitive and honest way that will help the child to understand the past while raising self-esteem, rather than making the child feel in some way responsible for the abuse or neglect, and lowering their feelings of self-worth.

Taking care to ensure that positive messages are there from the start, and threading them throughout the life story book, will begin to redress the unconscious negative feelings, and will help the child to challenge and reframe their limiting inner beliefs.

The subliminal messages throughout the child's book need to be:

- past events are not the child's fault

- he or she is loved and loveable

- he or she deserves better care and parenting

- he or she is claimed and belongs

- adults can be trusted and they understand.

The final message should be one of a positive and hopeful future.

CHAPTER 5

Involving Carers and Adoptive Parents

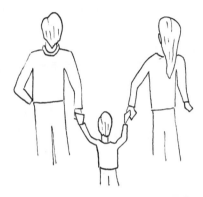

If carers and adoptive parents are to look after and re-parent their child successfully, with empathy and with an understanding of their child's 'inner world' and the impact this has on his or her current behaviour, then they will clearly need access to a very detailed history and a chronology. Although written for the child, a carefully prepared life story book will also help those caring for the child to see the child's story from a different perspective: the child's. 'Sharing this information and discussing it with the parents can also be a therapeutic experience for them, such that it gives them insight into their child and a greater sense of empathy' (Burnell and Vaughan 2008, p.228).

To use the book appropriately, carers and adoptive parents need to appreciate its purpose and to understand the significance of those important subliminal messages. If they have had the opportunity to contribute and to suggest amendments to the final version, they will feel more comfortable with the content and therefore more confident about using the book. In essence, the book needs to be both child and carer or adopter friendly!

The importance of involving adopters is now acknowledged in statutory guidance: 'It is important therefore for [the book] to be written in a simple and age-appropriate style and that the language and terms used are agreed with the prospective adopter before the book is handed over' (Department for Education 2013, p.107). This should apply to all permanent carers.

Furthermore, in England, the timing for the completion of the life story book reflects this different perspective. Rather than at time of placement, new Department for Education guidance, issued originally in 2011, states that, 'The completed life story book should be presented [to the adoptive parent] within ten working days of the adoption ceremony, i.e. the ceremony to celebrate the making of the adoption order' (2013, p.107).

It is imperative that the carers and adoptive parents feel able to share the important 'middle' section – the history – with their child. If they seem reluctant to read about the past with the child, this may give the impression that there is something so awful and bad in the past that the child will not be able to cope with it. In fact, whatever the past, the child has already lived through it and survived. What is sharable is bearable.

On some level, whether conscious or unconscious, the child is likely to have memories of their early neglect or abuse. Not acknowledging this could feed the child's sense of shame and increase their fear of further rejection if their 'awful secret' is discovered.

The adults caring for the child can feel confident that recalling a painful past in a safe, trusted and nurturing environment will not re-traumatize the child. On the contrary, it reassures the child that the adults already know all about them – including their past – and that they still find them loveable.

The content of the book is obviously important, but the actual process of telling the story can also help with the attunement and attachment processes. The carer or adoptive parent's tone of voice, facial expressions and body language will all have an impact on the child. Simple clip art illustrations of different facial expressions can be included to allow the adult and child to gently and playfully explore the links with different feelings and emotions. This is of particular significance as many children have great difficulty 'reading' faces.

For young children, the carer or adopter may read only a few of the words and the child will be more interested in the illustrations, scanned photographs and captions. Later the words, and the feelings behind them, will become more significant.

The book may provoke a mixture of emotions for both child and adult – providing an opportunity that could be used to good effect by an attuned and empathetic carer and adoptive parent.

CHAPTER 6

Compiling a Life Story Book

Remember that other reports and documents should be available to the child at a later stage. The life story book is just the first tool used to help the child to understand his or her self and history.

There are a number of points to consider when writing a life story book:

- Historical details are available from the child's file, from previous foster carers and from members of the birth family. Current information should be gathered from the carers or adoptive parents and from the child. Check names and terms used by the child and family. A simple checklist can be completed with or by previous foster carers, current carers or adopters before you begin. Significant facts and information about the birth family would have been gathered for the various court documents and for panel papers, but there may still be opportunities to check these details and to gather 'soft' information, e.g. favourite colour or food, shoe size, etc. before the book is finalized. Many birth parents contest care and adoption proceedings and may have been reluctant to disclose such information at that time. Some may be more willing to engage, and to contribute to the book at this later stage. This is now for the child's benefit. (See Appendices A, B and C.)

If old enough, let the child choose a title for the life story book – 'All About Danny', 'Danny Rules OK', 'Cool Dude Danny' and 'Danny's Life Adventure' are just some of the suggestions received from children. Put the year on the title page too.

Encouraging the child to choose the title, suggesting that they decorate the front cover of the folder or, if printing and binding the book, allowing them to select the photograph or illustration they would like you to use on the front cover, engages the child in a fun and very non-threatening way and helps him or her to claim the book and the story as theirs. If the child is too young to have any direct input the carer or adopters may have some ideas – and may be more artistic, more creative and have more IT skills than many of the professionals. Indeed, some of the most attractive books have been created by the carers and adopters.

- The book is not an abridged version of the child's permanence or placement report. It must be child focused and child friendly and contain bite sized sections, with scanned photographs and plenty of colour, bright borders, drawings and clip art to illustrate activities, events and feelings and to break up the text. Include playful elements and for very young children think about using images of footprints (or teddies, mice, frogs, etc.) on each page and inviting the child to follow those images throughout the story.

Social work jargon, such as 'placed on the Child Protection Register under the category of emotional neglect', is meaningless to a five-year-old or indeed to the average adult! Imagine reading the story aloud. The book needs to engage the child from the start. It should flow. Keep the child firmly in mind as you write.

- The book needs to be child sized – in other words, not so large and heavy that it is difficult for a young child to lift or hold. It also needs to be durable and child proof. Laminating the pages may seem appropriate for toddlers, but this tends to make the book very heavy. A spare copy or an electronic version may be the solution.

- Use the child's first name and write in the third person, unless working with older children who are writing the story with you. For younger children, the less direct approach is a more effective and less threatening way of exploring their history. Toddlers use their names rather than 'I' or 'me' and only gradually develop a sense of self. Many children function at a very young emotional age, and carers and adopters are encouraged to 'think toddler'. Using the third person in the book mirrors this developmental process, and young children love to see their name in print. An eight-year-old counted the number of times his name appeared so that this information could be added to the content page of his book. It was the start of engagement and meant that he had at least looked at every page.

- Despite recent initiatives to increase the number and range of children adopted from care, the average age of children being adopted in the UK is still under four years old. Irrespective of age, when preparing the book, you should make it appropriate for a school-age child (roughly five to ten years old). They may already have gone through the book many times, but it is only when they start school that children begin to understand the emotional significance of their adoption. Prior to this some will assume that, just like them, everyone has been fostered and adopted.

The majority of children placed permanently with long-term foster carers or Special Guardians are under ten years old and a study undertaken by Harwin and colleagues (2016, p.5), looking specifically at Special Guardianship Orders, showed that over 60 per cent of these children were under five years old, so this approach would also be suitable for this cohort of children.

For older children in care, a summary of their history, similar to the later life letter prepared for adopted children, may be more appropriate than a life story book, although some teenagers may still welcome this or may prefer an electronic version. Hammond and Cooper (2013) provide a comprehensive guide to engaging young people by using technology – computers, camcorders, sound tracts, photo-collages and smart phones – to create digital life story books.

- A school project about families and requests for baby photographs raises many issues for children who do not live with their family of birth. Changes in the way thoughts are processed are also occurring at this age, which can lead to further questions.

Carers or adoptive parents who have been looking after their children since they were babies or toddlers often notice a change around the age of eight or nine. Some sense an undercurrent of sadness or grumpiness, while others comment on increased concerns, difficulties, lethargy, anger or aggression. 'Attachment issues' become more apparent, and carers or adopters may feel confused and ineffective, as they begin to absorb the child's emotions.

It is at this stage that a carer or adoptive parent will be able to use a sensitively written life story book to most effect. While reminding the adults about the child's history, it can also be used to reassure the child and to help unravel the confused thoughts and emotions they are struggling to understand, and is an opportunity to revisit, redress any misconceptions and build on the information in the book.

The format: Present → Past → Present → Future

- Beginning the story with the child's birth and with the birth parents' details and history will be overwhelming and is not a good way to promote a secure attachment between the carer or adopters and child. For adopted children, a photograph, often taken on the maternity ward, of 'Mummy' holding the newborn, and placed on the opening page of the book, feels insensitive. It is a difficult place to start and confusing for the young child. The adopter is beginning by reminding the child that he or she is not actually 'Mummy' or 'Daddy'. Think of the subliminal messages here, for both child and adopter, about being claimed and being allowed to claim.

  Helping the child to feel safe, contained and 'grounded' in the present is a more appropriate starting point. From this position the carer or adoptive parent can help the child to look back and begin to make some sense of their history.

- To understand ourselves fully and move on to the future we need to understand our past, but young children live very much in the present and have a limited understanding of 'yesterday' or 'tomorrow'. Many older children have a similarly fragile grasp of time, so first we need to give them a much stronger sense of their present.

1. Present

- Start the book with the present: the child as he or she is now, with scanned photographs of the child, the current family and the home.

- Include a general description, some photographs of the child, and at least one of the child with the carers or adopters and other family members. They should feature at the beginning and not be tacked on, almost as an afterthought, at the end. Include family pets.

    For children living permanently with relatives or with foster carers check on preferred names. For instance some children refer to and feel more comfortable introducing their foster carers as aunty or uncle. For adopters, do not refer to them as 'new' Mummy or Daddy – just as Mummy or Daddy, and do so throughout the book.

- Make sure there are many positive comments about the child right from the start. For example, sparkly/twinkling eyes, lovely/sunny smile or soft/shiny hair. The carers or adopters need to be very involved, so include positive comments from them about the child and his or her talents, interests, nicknames, etc. – and interweave these positives throughout the body of the book.

    Be mindful of the subliminal messages. Children need to feel positive about themselves – that they are valued, loveable and loved.

- If the child is at nursery or school, add a few comments and pictures and mention names of teachers, pick out any positive comments they have made, and mention favourite subjects and names of friends.

    If children are struggling with school there will still be positive comments to include. They may be great at helping the teacher to put things away, or good at cutting and sticking, kind to other children or amazing at cartwheels! Feed the positives and don't dwell on the negatives. The life story book is not the place for this!

- For children who find separations difficult, carers and parents may find that they are frequently asked to collect the children early from school, either because they are upset, feeling ill, or they have been disruptive in some way. Children express separation anxiety in many different ways and this issue could be alluded to indirectly by mentioning that while the child is at school his mum and dad still think about him as they are cleaning the house, shopping, working at the office, etc. Out of sight is not out of mind – and this needs to be constantly reinforced in all kinds of ways. Children need to feel that they are held in mind by the adults and will not be forgotten.

- Write about the child's name and scan in a copy of the short birth certificate. If the book is for an adopted child this will be the new certificate showing the adoptive names. If the certificate has not been processed in time, use a simple illustration. Most adopters will add at least one new middle name and occasionally, if the first name is very unusual and there are serious risks to the placement stability from the birth family, adopters may be advised to change this name too. Mention the meaning or significance of current names.

  For an adopted child, this could lead to a simple explanation about the change to the child's birth name, but with the rise in social networking sites and the need for confidentiality, be cautious about including the child's original surnames, or any other identifying information, in the book. Many professionals struggle with this and feel that whatever the age and whatever the circumstances the child has the right to know these details. This is their information, but it may be more appropriate to share it at a later stage. We must consider any potential risks to a child's security, now and well into the future. The duty of care does not end with the adoption order.

Some children will of course already know their birth surname, so you may wish to include it, but even then, remember that the child may show the book to friends, relatives or teachers, so it may still be unwise to include any identifying third party information. Knowing something and committing it to print are not the same.

Children in care and those who are adopted can be very vulnerable. Many have poor impulse control and can't easily see the consequence of their actions. They may need some protection. Fursland (2013) highlights the dangers of children contacting members of their birth family too easily and before they are ready, via Facebook, and warns of the emotional upheaval and damage this can cause if the child is not well prepared.

Helping the child to understand their early history can be achieved without including identifying information. These details will be well documented in other reports and can be included in the later life letter or in a summary and shared with the young person when they are of an age to fully understand the implications and any risks identified should they wish to go online and trace members of their birth family.

The Department for Education also recognizes these concerns and the statutory guidance notes that: 'Consideration should be given on whether the surname of the birth parents, family and others should be included in the life story book' (July 2013, p.107).

For children in other forms of permanent care there may not be the same issues of confidentiality regarding the birth surname, as this will usually be the name the child continues to use. If there are no concerns then it may be appropriate to scan in a copy of the full birth certificate, but there needs to be a risk assessment in all instances.

- Introduce the concept of families and how they are formed. For example, children join families in different ways: some are born into them, some are fostered and some are adopted, some live with Special Guardians, etc.

- If giving examples of other people who have been in care or adopted, make these meaningful to the child. For older children, Eddie Murphy, Steve Jobs, Nelson Mandela, Kate Adie or Fatima Whitbread may be appropriate, but these will mean little to younger children. For a four- or five-year-old, Superman, Stuart Little the mouse, Babe the pig, or Paddington Bear will have far more of an impact. Check with carer or adopters, as they will know who may be of significance for the child. Bring in positive examples of relatives or friends within the carer or adoptive parents' network who were also fostered or adopted. Think about the child's world and reinforce their own points of reference.

    For inter-country adoptions, there is often very little background information available and for some children who are 'abandoned' and their births not registered by birth parents, there is nothing, However the same format is still helpful and an honest but sensitive explanation is still needed.

2. Past

- Having explored and endorsed the present for the child, it is now time to introduce the past. Start with the beginning: the child's birth.

- If there is little information about the birth, use some poetic licence – generally we can assume that babies were born gorgeous, lovely, adorable, loveable little bundles. Details of birth weight and length, and time and day of birth are usually available for all domestic adoptions and should be included. If not easily obtainable, check with health visitors, GPs or try hospital archives. If the child was premature or unwell and in a special care unit, include details of this.

- All babies have a birth mother and a birth father, so simply say this. Again, for adopted children and possibly for some in permanent care, because of social networking and associated risks, it may be advisable to only give the birth mother's first name and, if known, the birth father's first name. From then on refer to them using their names only. Similarly, giving a birth parent's year of birth or age at the time of the child's birth rather than specific dates may be sensible. For children not adopted check what terms they use when referring to their birth parents, for example Mum, Mam, Mummy, Dad, Papa, etc.

  Scan in one or two photographs if they are available. (The originals and other birth family photographs can be safely put in a separate photograph album.) There are a few cases where photographs of the birth parents should not be included in the book. For example, for children who have experienced extreme violence or sexual abuse, photographs may re-traumatize and not be appropriate.

- If the birth father's identity is not known or there is no information available, this must be acknowledged. Not mentioning a birth father could lead the child to believe the father is just so 'bad' he has to remain a secret, or perhaps he is well known and too famous to have disclosed his identity, or the child may grow up assuming that the foster or adoptive father is actually their birth father. For example:

  ○ All children have a birth mother and a birth father. John's birth mother is called Susan and this is usually shortened to Sue. John's birth father is called Nigel. Very little is known about Nigel. Sue said that he was about the same age as her but much taller, around 6ft. He had a medium build and brown hair. Nigel and Sue hadn't known each other for very long. Sue told him that she was going to have a baby, but their friendship ended a few months before John was born and he had moved away. Sue said that he was a lorry driver and he was from Wales. He may have gone back to that area to live, but she wasn't sure.

  Give basic details of significant members of the birth family: ages, physical descriptions, ethnic and cultural information, religion, personalities, occupations, interests, hobbies and talents. If the birth parents were in care themselves as children mention this but do not overload with intimate details of their history. Keep this section short.

- Most children who come into care, for whatever reason, were wanted and welcomed into the world by their birth parents. The birth parent would have felt love for the child and they may have registered the birth, and chosen a name with great care and for a particular reason. All this should be mentioned.

- There has been much debate about the difference between being 'loved' and being 'loveable' and some may feel that being told that a neglectful or abusive parent loved him or her will be very confusing for a child. However, many adopted children were wanted and loved by their birth parents and it would be wrong to deny this, even if those same parents were later unable to parent the child appropriately. We need to be more creative about the way we explain and explore the nature of love and parenting within life story books. Say that the birth mother loved the child but couldn't look after her, or wasn't well so couldn't look after her. But this alone is not enough of an explanation. There must be more.

- There needs to be a sensitive and honest account of the events and concerns leading to the child's relinquishment or removal from the birth parents. Neglect or abuse needs to be explained in a very simple and non-judgemental way. Comments about the birth mother's 'inability to meet your physical and emotional needs' will mean nothing to a child.

  For example, children understand their basic needs, such as the need for food and clothing, or to go to school, or for lots of cuddles and clean nappies as a baby. They need to know that their birth parents simply didn't know how to or were just not able to look after them properly, and certainly not in the way that such a precious and loveable child deserved.

- Giving an honest account of the circumstances leading to the child coming into care, while acknowledging sadness and loss, should make it clear that any neglect or abuse was not the child's fault. Words need to be carefully chosen to ensure that they do not feed into the child's sense of blame and shame.

- Lengthy accounts of the birth parents' unhappy childhood, and explanations of the 'root cause' of their difficulties, should not be in the child's book. You may want to add a simple explanation about why the birth parents struggled. For example, there could be learning difficulties, mental health issues, or it may be that when their birth mother or father were children, the adults didn't look after them in the way they should have, so as they grew up they didn't learn how to look after themselves very well and that made it very difficult for them to look after anyone else. Word this carefully, as it is very easy for children to feel somehow responsible for the birth parents' sadness or inadequacies, and still believe that as the abuse or neglect was not really their birth parents' fault, it must be theirs – again reinforcing their sense of 'badness'.

- Information about case conferences and reviews with specific dates is not needed. Keep these details for the later life letter and other reports that will be available to the child when they are older. They will over-complicate and actually detract from the child's understanding of their story.

    Mention going to the court and the judge being the important person who reads all the reports and listens to everyone, including the birth parents, and then makes big decisions about children and who should look after them. The judge grants the Care Order, Special Guardianship Order and in the case of adoption the Placement Order. If relevant, proposed contact arrangements could be included here, but keep it simple.

- Give information and photographs about the previous short-term foster carers – but again not too much, as children should now be given a memory book or photograph album capturing their time with the carers. If there were several fostering placements, this is usually due to the carers' other commitments, so choose words carefully to ensure that the child does not think that they were moved to other foster carers or to the adoptive parents for 'being naughty'.

- Bring the story back to the current family. 'Fostering Panels' or 'Adoption and Permanency Panels' and 'Matching Meetings' might be relevant for some children, but protracted explanations are not needed. There is usually a photograph of the child's first meeting with the carers or adopters and they themselves may have positive comments about this to quote in the book. Some say 'It was love at first sight' or 'I just knew that you were the child for me' and they may have another positive memory or anecdote to tell. Usually at this stage, the children in photographs look tense and anxious, so avoid captions about how happy and delighted the child was to meet their new family or to have a 'new mummy and daddy'. While it might be appropriate to comment on the adults' sense of joy, acknowledge the understandable ambivalence of the child. It is important for children to feel that they are loveable and loved, rather than feeling they must instantly love the adults.

  Birth parents often meet the carers or adopters before the child is actually placed with them, or shortly afterwards. Such meetings can be a positive experience for all and a photograph of this should be included in the life story book. It could convey a powerful message of the birth parents' sadness but also some acceptance and giving the child permission to join the new family.

- Give some details of the move to the new home, including how strange it must have been for the child at first. Comment on all the different things the child had to get used to – different people, a different house, a different bedroom, different food, different words for things, different smells and sounds, different feelings, different colours and furniture, different nursery/school and so on. So many differences!

- Comment on the foster carers' or adoptive parents' knowledge and understanding of the child, and how they knew about all the things needed to keep a child happy, healthy and safe. It may be appropriate to mention that they also realized that some of the child's previous experiences may have left him or her feeling worried, wobbly, upset, cross, angry or sad. This could provide an opportunity to explore facial expressions and feelings with the child.

- Writing the book in the third person also affords more opportunity for gentle or playful conjecture with regard to the child's emotions. 'I expect that John may have felt...' or 'I wonder if John felt...' or 'I wonder if you felt...', rather than writing in the first person. This allows for further discussion between the child and parent. The child can either identify with or reject the suggested feelings.

- If the child has particular problems, such as bed-wetting, nightmares or eating difficulties, this could be tentatively explored via the book – but never in direct reference to the child. For example:

> If children keep all their worries inside, their inside soon becomes so full it just can't hold them all in! These scary feelings can sometimes make children feel cross or grumpy, or all these worries can make children's tummies feel wobbly, or can give them tummy ache. Sometimes all their muddly feelings and thoughts just have to 'leak out'.
>
> If this happens at night when children are asleep, then some children may suddenly need to go to the

toilet, or if they are fast asleep they might wet their beds, or they could have muddly, scary dreams and wake up feeling very frightened.

All children can be helped so that their worries don't make them all wobbly inside and they don't 'leak out' in these ways.

If they just shared their worries with their mum, dad or another grownup they should soon find that their worries are just not so scary after all!

If John has any worries he just needs to share them with his mum and dad. They will understand and together they will be able to help him sort everything out.

If the child is familiar with, or has a favourite therapeutic story, you could playfully refer to this in the life story book, e.g. *A Nifflenoo Called Nevermind* (Sunderland 2001) for a child who bottles up feelings, or *No Matter What* (Gliori 1999) for a child who feels grumpy and fears being unlovable.

- Contact arrangements, whether direct or indirect, should be simply explained making it clear that this was the adults' decision. Children may have some involvement in the indirect contact (letterbox/information exchanges), but it is not their responsibility to write or to respond to letters from birth relatives. The arrangement is between the adults, and if any direct meetings are planned the carer or adoptive parents should be involved. A few photographs of recent contacts with siblings or other birth relatives should be included in the book.

- For adoptions, give details of the actual 'Adoption Celebration Day' and how this was celebrated, any comments the 'wise judge' made or thoughts he or she may have had!

For example, the judge also realized just how precious and loveable the child was and just how much the adoptive parents loved him or her. Again, scan in photographs.

- Do not end the book here!

3. Present

- Bring the child back to the present, with examples of how well the carers or adopters know and love them and mentions of everyday occurrences, activities and family rituals and routines, which will all help to 'ground' the child.

- Listing and illustrating some of the child's favourite things (e.g. favourite drink, food, colour, book, film, TV programme or toy) will demonstrate just how well the carers or adoptive parents know the child and may prove to be one of the child's favourite pages.

4. Future

- Finally, give the child a positive and compelling future – identify some plans and hopes. This could be planning to join the beavers/brownies or having swimming lessons next month or next year, or the long-term aspiration of becoming a gymnast, an astronaut or a train driver, or for one little girl it was to be 'an insect inspector'!

- End with a few photographs of life over the last year or so, with the carer or adoptive family, and by thinking about plans for next year, the year after and the year after that and so on, making it clear that the child's future is with this family, until they are grown up and, in the case of adoption, forever.

Children grasp the concept of 'forever' from a very young age. Many of the classic and much loved children's stories end with everyone living 'happily ever after'. Some practitioners are reluctant to use this term 'in case the adoption disrupts', as they feel that they cannot give the child this 'guarantee'. The decision to place a child for adoption is not made lightly and is rigorously and independently scrutinized, at every stage. If adoption is the agreed plan the child should be placed with conviction. The message that this is not yet another temporary placement should be loud and clear for the child, and when the Adoption Order is granted the expectation is that it will indeed be a 'happy ever after story' – that it will be forever!

Some adoptions do disrupt. Numbers are relatively low, they occur predominately during the challenging teenage years and the young person's mental health is usually the precipitating factor. Selwyn and colleagues' research confirmed this and she commented on the 'commitment and tenacity of adoptive parents' (2014, p.287). For those placements that had ended, many of the adoptive parents continued to support, albeit from a distance, and remained part of the young person's life, even if they could not live under the same roof. These adopters 'still saw themselves as the child's parents' (p.287). Furthermore, in the UK, an Adoption Order is irrevocable. A child may go on to be adopted by someone else, but this would be unusual, especially with teenagers, so unless this happens, the adoptive parent will be the child's legal parent forever.

Therefore, referring to adoptive families as 'forever families' seems accurate and appropriate. Reinforcing this at the end of the book gives a loud, clear and hopeful message to those young children.

The book doesn't have to be read in one session. If the child is very young, carers or adopters are not expected to read all of the words. Just pointing to some of the photographs and reading captions may be enough. Some children may only want to read the first and the last section, will skip over the important middle chapters, and may remain a little apprehensive about this part of the book for a while. That's okay. They are not ready yet, so allow them time. They will eventually be able to go through the entire book.

The life story book will be read to the child many times in the years to come, and will be the catalyst for further questions, explanations and numerous discussions as the child's level of understanding increases.

The child will obviously not remain at the age they were when the book was written, but the important information about when, why and how they joined the family, and the positive subliminal messages it contains, will not change. In this sense the book will 'stand the test of time' and will never be out of date. If the child, carer or adopter wishes to go on adding further information, this can easily be added at the end. The format lends itself to this.

CHAPTER 7

Sample Life Story Books

Children are unique, as are their stories, so no two books will be the same. It is not a case of 'one size fits all', but the following sample books may inspire further ideas. Note that they are written in the third person using 'child friendly' language, and contain positive subliminal messages throughout the 'bite sized' sections.

Danny's book contains a few simple illustrations. The other stories are text only, but suggestions for illustrations appear in italics throughout. The actual life story books should be bright and appealing. Use colourful borders, scanned photographs, plenty of illustrations and playful clip art on every page to break up the text and to hold the child's interest.

You may wish to present the final version in an album, a folder with plastic insets, or as a bound book. You should consider providing an electronic copy as well. Presentation will vary. Some services have access to a printing department and are able to produce a very 'professional' finish to the book, while others struggle with extremely limited resources and even accessing a colour photocopier is difficult. Taking into account financial constraints, there still seems little excuse for children's services not having appropriate resources to produce books that are 'fit for purpose' in terms of the content and presentation. The books must be appealing and child friendly.

All of the children in the sample books are fictitious but their stories may be familiar, as they are amalgamations of many children's stories:

Danny's Life Adventure: Danny is five years old and recently adopted, having lived with his adoptive parents for just over a year. His early life was quite chaotic. For much of the time, due to their alcohol and drug abuse, his birth parents were unavailable both emotionally and physically. He has two older sisters who provided some of the 'parenting', but from a very young age Danny learnt not to rely on the adults in his life and he became fairly self-sufficient. His sisters remain in foster care and Danny still has contact with them.

All about Angela: Angela is a one-year-old relinquished baby. Her birth mother was a student and she discovered that she was pregnant just after starting a university course. She met Angela's father at a party. She couldn't remember much about him or about the evening. She thought that she had too much to drink and may have passed out, or possibly that her drink had been 'spiked'. She planned to continue her education and felt that adoption would be the best option for the baby. Angela was fostered for several months before being placed with her adopters. The couple have an older daughter, also adopted.

Angela's book is far too detailed to be read in its entirety to a one-year-old, and at this stage adopters would only be expected to point to pictures and illustrations and use these to tell a simplified version of her story.

Here Comes Rosie: Rosie is seven years old and lives with her younger sister, Lily, at her paternal grandmother's home. The grandmother is Rosie's and Lily's Special Guardian. The family was known to the police and children's services, as there was a history of neglect and domestic violence.

The girls still have contact with their mother and father and with their two younger brothers, who have been adopted.

The history section is more detailed in this book. Rosie may wish to share this book with her birth parents at some stage, and the book provides an honest but non-judgemental account and acknowledges the sadness and loss that Rosie feels and the love that she has for them.

Tandi's Special Book: Tandi is nine years old and she lives with her older brother and is permanently placed with long-term foster carers. She has been here since she was seven years old and prior to this she lived in two different short-term foster homes. Tandi's mother has experienced periods of depression and she has had many hospital admissions due to mental health concerns. The birth parents' relationship was a turbulent one; Tandi's father left when she was two years old and his current whereabouts is unknown.

Tandi lacks confidence in her abilities and doesn't like much about herself physically either. While answering the what, why and when questions, the book also comments on her positive attributes and aims to gently raise self-esteem and playfully acknowledges that of course, Tandi may 'not agree'.

As with the others, this book is written in the third person but refers to 'you', instead of the child's name.

Kasem's Life Journey: Kasem is an inter-country adoptee. He is five years old and was born in Thailand and left outside a baby home. It is believed that both of his birth parents were Thai, but there is no other information. Kasem remained in the orphanage until he was 14 months old and then came to England with his adoptive parents. He was officially adopted in the UK about a year later. His adoptive parents subsequently adopted another child, also from Thailand.

Danny's and Tandi's stories can be found in this book. Angela's, Rosie's and Kasem's stories are available as downloadable content.

The sample life story books for
Angela, Rosie and Kasem can be accessed at:
www.jkp.com/voucher
using the code REESLIFESTORY.

Danny's Life Adventure 2017

Contents

1. All about Danny

Danny was born on 5 August 2011, so that makes him 5 years old at the moment. He is a fine looking boy with a lovely smile, sparkly brown eyes and short dark brown hair.

Danny is a bright, friendly, chatty boy and he is generally very cheerful and happy – and of course his mum and dad think that he is just lovely!

Danny is just about the right height and the right build for a 5-year-old. He is fit and healthy, with plenty of energy, so he is usually very busy. He loves cycling or scooting to the park at the end of his road with his mum and dad. Sometimes he meets his friends there and they play football, have running races or climb trees – and Danny loves to organize everyone! On sunny days they have a picnic or a barbeque and then Danny knows this is something that the grownups are in charge of!

Danny prefers to be outside but when indoors he likes to play with his dinosaur collection or his toy cars. He also likes drawing and painting. Sometimes he plays on the computer or watches television, but Danny doesn't like to sit still for too long. Of course, some quiet times are very good for any growing boy, so his mum is helping him with this. Now Danny really enjoys snuggling up on the settee, just the two of them, and having special story times.

2. Danny's Home and Family

Danny lives with his mum, his dad and his sister, Jane, in Newtown. They all live in a three-bedroomed house. Danny has his own bedroom — it's the one at the front in the photograph. He has dinosaur wallpaper, a dinosaur duvet cover, a dinosaur rug, a dinosaur lamp — and I think I can even see one of his dinosaurs peeping out of that window!

This is Danny with his mum and dad. His mum's name is Sandra and his dad is called Tom.

Danny's sister is Jane. Jane is four years older than Danny, so she is nine years old at the moment. Most of the time Danny and Jane play well together, but Mum says that sometimes they can have their 'off days' too. I wonder what she means?

Danny also has grandparents. There is Nana and Pops. That Mum's mum and dad. And there is Granny and Grandpa, and that's Dad's mum and dad. They live quite a long way away but sometimes they come to Danny's house for Sunday lunch or Danny goes to see them.

And finally, we mustn't forget the other member of the family – Tiger, the cat.

This is Danny with all of his family on holiday last year. They were on the beach in Devon.

This was Danny's first seaside holiday. He loved building sandcastles but the sea was just too cold! Danny thinks that swimming in a pool is much warmer, and his sister Jane agrees!

3. St Paul's School

Danny goes to St Paul's Infants School and his sister goes to the school next door – St Paul's Junior School. The schools are quite close to Danny's home, so he and Jane can scoot there and back every day. His mum always makes sure that they arrive in plenty of time in the morning. Every afternoon, when school finishes, Mum or Dad is waiting for him by the school gate, and then together they go to collect Jane from her school.

Last term Danny's teacher was Mrs Baker. She was a very nice lady, with lots of patience, so she didn't usually get cross with any of the children. Danny likes Mrs Baker because she smiles at him every morning and says, 'Hello Danny. How are you?' His teacher really likes Danny too, and told his mum that he is a lovely boy to have in the classroom and that she is really going to miss him next term when he moves to Mrs Jones' class. Luckily, Danny has heard that Mrs Jones is a very nice teacher too!

Danny is good at numbers and he likes art and computer work best. Some of his reading books and the spellings he had to learn last year were very hard, but he had a good school report and the teacher said that he always tries his best and works hard. Mrs Baker also said that Danny is now much better at asking the teacher for help when he doesn't quite understand what he has to do. He has a certificate for this. So well done Danny!

Perhaps the best part of school is playtime and then Danny can play football. Danny has lots of school friends. There is Fred, Toby, Owen, Wing, Jo, Grant, Kath and Sian – and there are a few others too. What a lot of different names!

4. Danny's Name

Danny's name is actually Daniel but he is usually called Danny – and he likes this. His full name is Daniel Anthony Davies and this is a copy of his birth certificate.

Of course, Danny's name was not always Daniel Anthony Davies. At first, it was just Daniel and he had a different surname. How can this be? Well, families come in all shapes and sizes and children join families in all sorts of ways. Some are born into them, some live with step parents or with aunts and uncles, grandparents or friends, or with Special Guardians. Some children live with foster carers, while some are adopted into their families.

Foster carers sometimes look after older children for a long time, but they usually only look after young children for a short while, either until they go home or until they move to a new family to be adopted. Adoption means that children stay with their new mum and dad until they are all grown up.

Many famous people and characters have been adopted, like Moses in the Bible, Superman, Stuart Little the mouse, Paddington Bear and Babe the pig. Danny's sister, Jane, is also adopted, his cousin Clive is adopted and there are many other adopted children living in Newtown and indeed all over the world! So, like thousands of other children, Danny was adopted and this is how Danny became:

Daniel Anthony Davies.

5. The Beginning

Danny was born on 5th August 2011, and like most babies he was born in hospital. He was born in West Hospital in London at 7.30 in the morning, so just in time for breakfast, and as it was summertime it was a nice warm day.

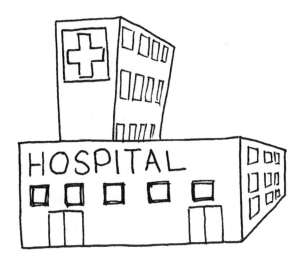

Danny weighed 2.5 kg, and that is 5.5 pounds or the same as two and a half bags of sugar. This is quite small for a newborn baby and so, for the first two weeks, Danny was in a special cot – an incubator – as he needed extra care.

The 5th August was a Friday, so according to the children's rhyme Danny is 'loving and giving'. The August flower is a gladiolus and the birth stone is peridot. This is a precious green gem.

Danny's birth sign is Leo, the lion. People with this birth sign are said to be generous, warm-hearted, kind and enthusiastic, but sometimes they can be a bit bossy too! I wonder if this sounds a bit like Danny?

Like all newborn babies, Danny had a birth mother and a birth father. Danny's birth mother is called Ann and his birth father is David. When Danny was born, Ann and David were very happy and they both thought that he was a lovely and very loveable baby, and they phoned their family and friends to let them know that their gorgeous baby boy had arrived.

They decided to name their baby Daniel. Ann chose the name Daniel as that was her grandfather's name.

Ann has brown eyes and when Danny was born she had long dark hair, but she later had it cut short and sometimes she changed the colour too. Ann was born in South London and she was 29 years old when Danny was born. She wasn't very tall — just over 5 ft — and she was slim, and sometimes she wore glasses. She liked school and had done well passing lots of exams. When she left she worked in an office for a while and then in a shop. Ann was a friendly lady and she enjoyed going out and dancing.

David was much taller than Ann — he was nearly 6 ft — and he was well built. He had light brown hair and blue eyes. David was born a year before Ann, so he was 30 years old when Danny was born. David was born in Liverpool but moved to London with his family when he was very young. David didn't enjoy school very much and when he left he started to train as a gardener as he liked being outside, but then he changed his mind and worked in a garage. When he was 19 years old, he started to work at a supermarket and this is where he met Ann.

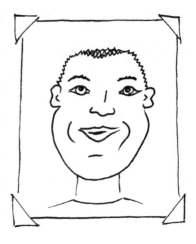

6. Staying with Alice and Ken

Ann and David decided to live together soon after they met and at first they were very happy. They were delighted when their first child, Laura, was born and when their second daughter, Jade, was born a year later, but gradually things started to go wrong. Ann and David were arguing too much and this must have been very scary for the girls. Sometimes David would get so cross he would lose his temper and then he would hurt Ann. Sometimes the neighbours heard the shouting and they would telephone the police. Then the police and the social workers would come to the house to calm everyone down, and to make sure that Laura and Jade were okay.

Perhaps it was because Ann and David were feeling unhappy that they began drinking cans of lager, as they thought that this would help. When this didn't make them feel any better they began taking drugs. Again, they thought that taking drugs would make them happier, but of course all it did was make everything much, much worse! In fact, sometimes the lager and the drugs made them feel very ill and very sleepy – and even more unhappy!

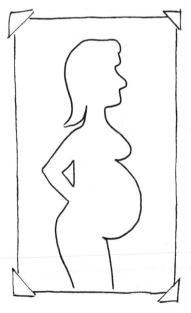

When Ann knew that she was going to have another baby she was very pleased, but sadly she was still taking some drugs, and this is why Danny needed special care when he was first born. The drugs that had sometimes made Ann feel unwell had also made little baby Danny feel ill while he was growing inside Ann. They also made him unwell when he was first born and he needed special medicine to help him feel better.

Thankfully Danny was soon well enough to leave hospital and the whole family were really pleased when he went home. Laura was 10 years old and Jade was 9 years old at that time, and although they were in school for some of the time, when they were home they liked helping Ann to look after baby Danny. Although they were only young children too, sometimes, especially when Ann and David were feeling ill, they would bath and feed the baby and put him to bed.

Danny had his first birthday and then his second birthday with Ann, David and his sisters, but by this time many people – the doctors, the health visitors, the teachers at Laura and Jade's school, the police and the social workers – were becoming very worried about all the children, but especially little Danny. Ann and David were not looking after him properly and not giving him all the time and attention that babies must have, so baby Danny just wasn't growing as much as he should.

In fact, Ann and David were not looking after any of the children very well. The home was dirty and messy, there were no clean clothes, the girls were missing lots of school because Ann and David didn't make sure that they were up in time in the mornings. Sometimes there was no food in the house so they were often very hungry. Perhaps instead of buying food Ann and David were using their money to buy drugs – and they cost a lot of money! So the grownups were just not looking after the children properly. This must have been very frightening and scary for all of them.

One day the social worker and the police called at the house and found the children on their own. The children were hungry, cold and dirty. Everyone agreed that it was just too dangerous for them to live with Ann and David any longer. Little Danny looked very ill and he had a big bruise on his head so he was taken to hospital, while Jade and Laura went to stay with a foster carer, Pam. Pam would look after them properly and make sure that they were safe.

At the hospital the doctors looked at Danny's head. Ann and David came to the hospital to see Danny too, but they didn't know how he had hurt himself. The police and social workers spoke to Ann and David and told them that they should never leave children in the house on their own, as this is very dangerous. Children need grownups to look after them all the time.

Danny stayed in hospital overnight to make sure that he was okay, and then he went to stay with foster carers too. He went to stay with Alice and Ken.

Alice and Ken had looked after lots of babies and little children and they took very good care of Danny. It must have been quite scary at first and I expect that he missed everyone. He was very pleased when Jade and Laura came to visit him with their foster carer and when the social worker, Jaz, would come in her car and take him to the play room at the Children's Centre to see Ann and David every week.

At the foster home Danny grew really quickly. He put on weight and became much taller, and he really liked playing with Sam and Sally. Sam and

Sally were twins, and they had been living with Alice and Ken for quite a long time. Danny was sad when the time came for them to leave, but Alice and Ken told him not to worry because the twins were very pleased to be moving to a new family all of their own — an adoptive family.

7. Building Strong Walls

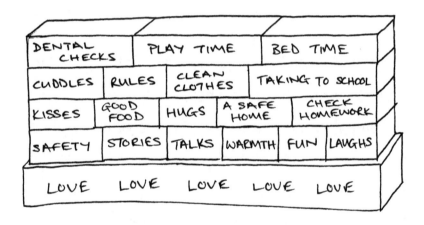

Bringing up children is a bit like building a wall. To make tall, strong walls you need a very good foundation and then, using just the right type and just the right amount of cement, you carefully lay all the different bricks on top. The cement is like the love that holds everything else together and makes the wall strong. You can see from this wall of bricks that children need love, but they also need lots of different kinds of caring to help them grow properly, and they need to be cared for by grownups who can make sure that the children are happy, healthy and safe.

Ann and David loved all of their children, but they were not able to look after themselves properly or do all the other things that parents must do to keep their children safe and to help them grow into strong, healthy grownups.

While the children were being cared for at their foster homes, the social workers and the doctors tried to help Ann and David. If they could stop taking drugs they might be able to look after their children again, but sadly this was too hard for them and although they tried, neither of them seemed able to do this.

The social workers had lots of meetings and long talks about Danny, Laura and Jade. No one thought that they should go back to Ann and David, so they went to the court to see the judge. Judges are very clever and very wise. The judge listened to everyone – to all the workers and to David and Ann. The judge agreed that the children should not live with their birth parents because they just didn't know how to look after them. The judge also thought that as Laura and Jade were older they should stay with their foster carer, Pam.

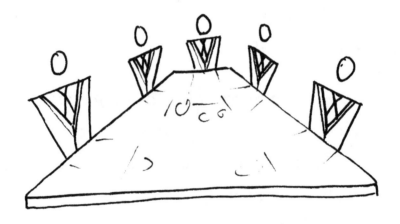

As Danny was so young, the judge felt that he needed a new family – one with a mum and dad who would be able to understand Danny and would know just how to look after him and keep him safe for a very, very long time – until he was all grown up!

Everyone thought that when Danny moved to his new family, he should still see Laura and Jade sometimes, but he wouldn't go to the Children's Centre to see Ann and David any more. Ann and David still cared about Danny and they wanted to know that he was well and happy, so it was also agreed that his new mum and dad could write to Ann and David and sometimes send some photographs to them, so that they would know that Danny was okay and growing into a fine boy. In turn, Ann and David could write to Danny's mum and dad to share their news.

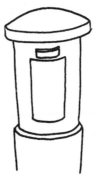

8. The Davies Family

Sandra and Tom were just the right grownups to be Danny's mum and dad. They knew what to do to help him to grow into a healthy, strong child – just like that strong brick wall. They knew that children need lots of love and cuddles, plenty of sleep and good food, a warm house, clean clothes, lots of fun, games and playtimes, and just the right number of rules to make sure that they are safe and secure.

Sandra and Tom fell in love with Danny as soon as they saw him. You could say that it was 'love at first sight'. They were so happy, although Danny was a little worried and looked very unsure at first. They gave him a very soft, furry toy puppy dog. Danny was only little and he couldn't say puppy at that time, so he called it 'putty' instead. Putty has had lots of cuddles from Danny since then and although he is not quite so furry now he still sits at the end of Danny's bed every night.

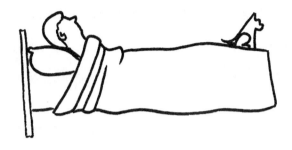

Sandra and Tom visited Danny every day after this and sometimes Jane came too. On one of the days, Jade and Laura arrived with their foster carer, Pam. They all exchanged presents and had a special tea party. Danny's mum and dad were pleased to meet them and Jade and Laura were very pleased to meet Danny's mum and dad too and they took lots of photographs.

Alice told Danny's mum and dad all about him and about the things he liked doing and eating, and what time he went to bed and what time he got up, and what he liked to have for breakfast. There was a huge list of things – likes and dislikes – and then, when everyone had got to know each other really well, Alice and Ken packed up all of Danny's things and helped his mum and dad to put them all into their car. It was quite a squash! Then Mum, Dad, Jane and Danny drove all the way from London to Newtown – and that's quite a long way, over 100 miles.

So Danny joined the Davies family at the beginning of 2015, when he was 3½ years old, and that was how Danny became Sandra and Tom's son, and how they became his mum and dad.

Of course it was very strange for Danny when he first moved to his new home. Danny had to get used to the new house: the rooms looked different, the furniture was different, the smells were different, his clothes felt different, the food was different, there were different Davies ways of doing things — they even had different words for some things — and he had a new sister, Jane! What a lot of different things for a little boy to get used to!

At first it must have been very strange, confusing and perhaps a bit worrying for Danny. His mum and dad could understand all this and they knew that, in time, with their love and care they would help Danny to feel safe, settled and loved.

Of course it must have been a bit worrying for Jane too. She had been adopted into the Davies family when she was 2 years old. Some children worry about having a new brother or sister and think that perhaps their mum and dad will not love them as much. I wonder if Jane worried about this too? Of course she needn't have worried! Jane and Danny's mum and dad have very big hearts and their love just keeps on growing and growing and growing so there will always be plenty of love for both of them.

9. The Wise Judge

After Danny had lived with his mum and dad for quite a long time, and when everyone knew each other very well, the social worker went to Court to see the judge again. She told him all about Danny and his family and he read lots of reports about Danny, his mum and dad and sister and about Ann and David and he said that Danny should definitely be adopted and he granted an Adoption Order.

A few weeks later, they all went to the court to see that very wise judge. All of the Davies family went. Mum, Dad, Jane and the social worker, Liz, and of course the most important person that day –

Danny. It was a very special occasion and everyone had the day off work and school to be there.

They all went to see the wise judge in the Newtown Court a few weeks before Danny's 5th birthday. The judge had already read all about Danny, and he knew just how loveable and precious he was and he said that Danny deserved loving, caring parents and he could see that Mum and Dad loved him very much. So the judge said again that Danny should definitely be adopted, and remain part of the Davies family forever.

Mum and Dad liked the name Anthony so they told the judge that they would like this to be Danny's new middle name. The judge liked the name too and he agreed and he signed the special certificates and Danny officially and legally became Daniel Anthony Davies.

This was called the Celebratory Adoption Hearing – and that's exactly what everyone did;

they celebrated!

They caught the train to London and they went on the London Eye.

Afterwards they had a special meal with Granny and Grandpa, and Nana and Pops.

10. More about Danny

Danny has been living with his mum and dad for quite a long time now and every day he is growing taller and stronger. He is a very important member of the Davies family and although he can still be a bit bossy at times he is beginning to realize that his mum and dad are very good at organizing everything and doing all the things that grownups should do to keep him safe. Most importantly, Danny's mum and dad know him so well, they understand him, they look after him, they know just what he needs, and they love him dearly...

In fact Danny's mum and dad know all sorts of very important things about Danny. For instance, they know that Danny's:

Favourite football club is Arsenal

Favourite TV programme is Scooby-Doo

Favourite book is Horrid Henry

Favourite food is Mum's sponge cake and her roast chicken dinner

Favourite drink is banana milkshake

Favourite colour is red

Favourite bedtime is being tucked in very tightly by Mum and having a bedtime story.

So, you can see Danny's mum and dad certainly know lots and lots about Danny!

Danny is still a very busy boy with plenty of energy and he has lots of plans for the future too. He is having another holiday this summer. The Davies family will be going to the seaside in Devon again. I wonder if the sea will be any warmer this year? Mum says that perhaps next year they might go to Spain for their holiday as the sea is very blue and very warm there, so Danny likes the sound of that!

Danny, Mum, Dad and Jane will be going to see Jade, Laura and Pam again soon. They are all going bowling and for a meal afterwards! Danny hopes it will be a hamburger! I wonder? And then, when

Danny goes back to school he will have swimming lessons and he is also going to join the cubs with his friends, Toby and Owen, so that will be more fun!

When he is grown up, Danny thinks he would like to be a footballer or a dog walker or he might like to fly an airplane! He is not quite sure yet, so he could change his mind about this. I wonder?

But there are some things that I certainly don't need to wonder about!

I just know for sure that whatever Danny does in the future his mum and dad will always be there to help him, to guide him and to love him. They will always be his mum and dad, and Danny will always be their very, very precious son...

forever and ever and ever...

Tandi's Special Book 2017

Contents

1. Here's Tandi

[Use a combination of scanned photographs, colourful clip art and borders to illustrate and to break up the text throughout the book.]

You were born in 2008, so you will have your 9th birthday this year. Everyone who knows you says that you are a very pretty girl with a great smile, big brown eyes, a lovely brown complexion and dark curly hair, which you usually wear in braids. You have lovely thick hair, although I wonder if you will agree!

A happy looking Tandi.

You are usually very chatty and bubbly and you like giving and receiving big hugs. You are tall and slim and you are certainly a very fit, healthy girl with plenty of energy. You are really good at gymnastics and athletics, although I wonder if you will agree!

Most of the time you are very cheerful, but just like everyone else, your moods can change and sometimes you can feel a bit grumpy and can look quite cross, especially when you are tired or hungry – I wonder if you will agree!

… and here you are pulling your grumpy face.

You like being outside in the fresh air playing football or running around or cycling or doing gymnastics, and you *do* especially impressive summersaults and handstands! You really like your scooter and you can do some tricks on the skateboard ramps in the local park.

In fact, you are so very talented in so many ways. You like making models and drawing pictures and painting. You are good at art although, once again, I wonder if you will agree!

With all of these interests, you don't have time to watch much television, but at the moment one of your favourite programmes is Dr Who.

2. Tandi's Home

This is your home and you have lived here for just over a year.

You and your brother Jordon, who is just 1 year older than you, live with your foster family in Croydon, South London. In the family there are your foster carers, Sharon and Pete, and their two teenage boys, Sam and Joshua, and you and Jordon.

This is Sharon and Pete.

Here you are with your brother and your foster brothers. Sometimes you all get on very well together and there is plenty of fun and laughter, but at other times you just don't, and then you really get on each other's nerves and you say that although all the boys are older than you, they can be 'very childish and a bit of a pain'. Sharon says that at times it can be a very noisy household and she could do with some earplugs!

And here's the entire family.

And here you are with Jordon when you were very little. So cute.

And here you are a bit older, before you came to live in South London.

Your family live on an estate with lots of similar houses and it is quite a busy place. You like this as you think that there is always something going on. There are lots of shops in the main part of the town and there is also a park just opposite your house and that's a great place to play football, ride your bike and there is the skate park too.

You have your own bedroom. It's not a very big room, but it is a nice, cosy room. The walls are blue and the curtains are bright yellow, which is your favourite colour at the moment, and you have just had a new bright blue duvet cover with yellow stars on it.

Your cosy bedroom.

Your foster carers really enjoy having you as part of the family. Sharon says it is so nice to have another girl in the house and she says that you are generally a very helpful and cheerful girl – I wonder if you will agree!

3. Tandi's School

This is your school.

You attend Fern Green Junior School. The school is quite close to your home. It's about a 20-minute walk, but sometimes Sharon drives you and your brother Jordon there – especially if it is pouring with rain or if you are running a bit late in the morning, as Sharon knows that you just hate being late.

Last year your teacher was Mr Moore. You were not in his class for long as you had only just moved to Croydon. This year your teacher is Mrs Khan. There are some things about school that you don't like, but you liked Mr Moore last year and he was very pleased with your progress and he said that you had worked very hard. In fact, Mrs Khan has also said that, 'there has been a very big improvement in Tandi's literacy skills this year'.

Congratulations on your good work.

A 'Well Done' certificate.

Like many children, you find some of the schoolwork difficult. Did you know that there are lots of very clever and very famous people who found schoolwork hard? Well there are!

At school you are generally well behaved and the teachers say that you always try your best and work hard. They agree that you are a bright child, but sometimes they say you 'lack confidence' — I wonder if you will agree!

The teachers agree that you are very, very, very good at sport and P.E. and your favourite subject at the moment is art and you also like doing projects. Your other lessons include maths, science, music, literacy, IT, French and geography.

These are some of the children at Fern Green School on their sports day.

You are in there somewhere.

You are popular and have plenty of friends at school, but you don't like all of the children in your class, just some of them. You think that some of them are a bit mean so you don't play with them. Your best friends are Betty, Molly and Grant.

Here you are with some of your friends.

4. Families

So you live in a house in Croydon with your brother and your foster family. You have lived here for the last year and you will be able to stay here until you are an adult. So how did all this come about?

Well, children join families in all sorts of ways. Some are born into them and live with a mum and a dad. Some have one mum, some have two, others have one dad or some have two dads. Some live with stepmums or stepdads, some live with aunts or uncles, grandparents or friends, and others live with foster carers, and some children are adopted or they have Special Guardians. So, basically, families are formed in many different ways and they come in all sorts of shapes and sizes!

If children can't live with any members of their born-to families, then foster carers will usually look after them, either for a short while, until they can go home again, or until they can move to a new long-term foster family or to an adoptive family. Long-term foster families and adoptive families are often called 'permanent families' as children usually live with them until they are grown up, or until they feel ready to leave and are old enough to look after themselves and want to have a home of their own.

So, like thousands of other children, you live with long-term foster carers. There will be many other fostered children in Croydon and all of Britain and indeed all over the world. Many famous people have been fostered, like Nelson Mandela, the ex-Prime Minister of South Africa, and Eddie Murphy, the actor.

As well as your brother Jordon, you also know some other people who are adopted or fostered. In fact, you recently went to a Fostering Network Family Fun Day at a country park and met lots of other children who were all fostered.

At first you lived with your born-to family, then with two short-term foster families before you came to live with Sharon and Pete, your long-term foster family. That's quite a lot of changes and moves for a young girl to deal with and it must have been very confusing and scary for you at times.

So why and how did all of this happen?

5. The Beginning

Like most babies, you were born in hospital. You were born on the 15th July 2008, in Hammersmith. You were born in West London Hospital, in the Princess Anne Ward. It was a summer's evening, and it had been a lovely sunny day.

[Baby photograph if available or use appropriate clip art.]

You were a gorgeous, loveable little bundle, although I wonder if you will agree!

You were a small baby, and the doctors thought that you had arrived early, which means that you were born several weeks before the date you were expected. You weighed 1.8 kg, which is the same as saying you weighed just over 4 pounds, so you were about the same as two bags of sugar, and this is quite light for a newborn baby.

You were born at 19.12, which is the same as 12 minutes past 7 o'clock in the evening.

It was a Tuesday, and there is a rhyme all about being born on different days of the week:

Monday's child is fair of face,

Tuesday's child is full of grace,

Wednesday's child is all aglow,

Thursday's child has far to go,

Friday's child is loving and giving,

Saturday's child works hard for a living,

But the child that's born on the Sabbath day is bonny and blithe, and good always.

So according to the rhyme, you are a very graceful person – so perhaps that is why you are so good at gymnastics! I wonder if you will agree!

Your Zodiac sign is Cancer, the crab, and your birth stone is a ruby and on the day you were born, Gordon Brown was the Prime Minister of the country.

6. Tandi's Mum and Dad

Like all babies you have a born-to mum and a born-to dad. Your birth mother is called Tania, and your birth father is called Dennis.

This is you and your mum shortly after your birth.

And here's your dad giving you a cuddle.

Your dad came to see you in hospital, just after you were born, and he was very proud of you and thought that you were just beautiful.

In fact, your mum and dad both thought that you were so lovely and they decided to name you Tandi. Your mum said it would be nice for mother and daughter to have similar names and Tandi is a Jamaican name and it means 'beloved' so she thought it was just right for her much loved baby daughter. Your dad chose your middle name, Rose, as this was his grandmother's name. He went with your mum to register your birth and you have his surname.

So your full name is Tandi Rose Watkins.

A copy of your birth certificate.

[You could scan copy of the full birth certificate, but if there are any concerns re confidentiality and social networking, then I suggest you scan in

a copy of the short certificate, without the birth parents' addresses.]

At the time of your birth, your mum had dark brown, shoulder length curly hair, but she later had it cut in a very short style. She has brown skin and you look quite like your mum and you have the same lovely complexion, although your skin tone is a little lighter. Your mum was born in Jamaica in 1982, so she was in her mid 20s when you were born. She is slim and 5ft 6in tall and she wears size 5 shoes and she likes wearing casual clothes, usually leggings or jeans.

Her family had lived in Jamaica for many generations. Her mother and father, Maria and Sam, and her grandparents, Grace and Jo, were all from there. You have a few photographs of Jamaica and of these relatives in your special photograph album.

Your mum left Jamaica when she was just 16 years old and made the long journey to the UK. The flight took about 12 hours and when she arrived she said that she was very tired and thought that the UK was very cold, but she was also very excited. She went to live with her Aunty Maria in Hammersmith. Her aunty was a nurse and Tania had planned to carry on her studies and train as a nurse too, but this didn't happen. Tania didn't really get on with her aunty and her aunty didn't like many of her friends and she especially didn't approve of her boyfriend at that time, as she felt that he was too old for Tania, as he was in his 30s.

Before long your mum left her aunty's house and moved into her boyfriend's flat, but things didn't work out very well for them and after a few months they separated. Your mum didn't have a job and she said that she was homeless for a while and then she lived in various hostels in the London area. She became quite depressed and she wasn't looking after herself very well. She wasn't washing and she wasn't eating much and after a while, the thoughts and the feelings inside her head became very confused and muddled.

When your mum was 19 years old she was admitted to hospital. Some people are admitted to hospital when they are very ill – perhaps they have a disease or a chest infection, or perhaps they have broken something, like a leg or an arm. These are all called physical illnesses or injuries. But sometimes people go to hospital because it is their minds that have become ill or broken, and this is called mental illness. This is what happened to your mum, and this is why her thoughts had become so jumbled. She stayed in hospital for several months, until she felt better, and the mental health social worker at the hospital helped her to find somewhere to live when she was discharged.

Your mum met Dennis, your dad, in a pub in Hammersmith a few years later. They started chatting, liked each other and started going out together and it wasn't long before they moved into a flat together.

Your dad had been a soldier in the army and when he left he started working in a warehouse in London and as a delivery man. He is tall, 6ft, and well built, with size 11 feet. He has red hair and he kept it very short and sometimes he shaved it off completely. He has a pale, freckled complexion and as he was born and brought up in Birmingham, he has a strong Birmingham accent. He was 10 years older than your mum, so she thinks that he was born in 1972. He liked playing computer games and watching TV.

Your mum said that she and your dad were happy for several years, but then things started to go wrong and there were lots of arguments and difficulties. They stayed in the Hammersmith area, but they moved around a lot and sometimes they were homeless or they stayed for a while with friends or relatives. At different times they were also both in trouble with the police and were arrested for fighting; your dad spent a few months in prison and Tania had more periods of depression and hospitalization.

Nevertheless they stayed together and your mum and dad had their first child, Jordon, in 2007. By then the health visitors and the social workers in Hammersmith were often visiting the family as they were very worried about the new baby. Sometimes your mum and dad would argue and shout in front of the baby and they would become violent and end up hurting each other and your mum would become depressed again.

On one visit the police went to the flat with the social worker and they said that the flat was cold and all of the curtains were closed, and although the flat was very dark, they could see that it was very dirty and in a terrible mess, with rubbish piled up on the floor and mouldy dishes in the kitchen. The social worker said that there was no food in the cupboards and they worried that your mum and dad were just not able to look after the baby properly. Your dad was no longer working, so money was tight, but instead of buying food for themselves and things that the baby needed, it seemed that your dad was using most of their money to buy alcohol – usually beer and lager. Perhaps he thought that drinking lots of alcohol would make him feel happier but it just seemed to make him more argumentative and it made everything much, much worse!

Things became so worrying that in February 2008, before you were born, and when Jordon was still only a baby, the police, the health visitors and the social workers all felt that it was now becoming an emergency. It was just too dangerous for the baby to stay with your parents as they felt he was being neglected. Jordon was 8 months old and he wasn't putting on any weight and he looked thin and ill.

Your mum and dad didn't agree and the social worker said that she would apply for an Emergency Order from the Court so that Jordon could be taken to a safe place. Your mum and dad were very angry with everyone at first, but then they agreed that it might be best if the baby went to a foster carer for a while, just to give them time to sort themselves out. So that is what happened. The social worker collected the baby and took him to stay with a foster carer called Julie.

Meanwhile, when the foster carer was looking after Jordon, the social workers, doctors and the health visitor tried to help your parents. If your dad could stop drinking so much alcohol they thought that he would be able to help your mum more and she would not get so depressed.

By this time your mum was pregnant again and you were on the way, so it was even more important that they sorted themselves out and they needed to get the flat ready. You were born 4 months after Jordon had gone to live with his foster carer and everyone agreed that it would be best if Jordon stayed with his foster carer for a little longer, until you were settled.

You stayed in the special care unit for a few weeks after your birth, just until you had put on some weight. By then your dad said that he was no longer drinking and he cleaned up the flat, so when you were ready to be discharged you went home with your mum and dad.

7. The Early Years

A month after you left hospital, Jordon came home too and you both lived with your mum and dad in the flat in Hammersmith for the next few years. Several different social workers and health visitors called at the flat to make sure that you and Jordon were okay and to check that you were growing and putting on weight in the way that you should.

Things seemed okay again for a few years, although the social workers were still worried about you sometimes. You and Jordon went to Happy Days Nursery most days, and the carers there would make sure that you were ok and you had plenty to eat while you were there.

This is the nursery.

Sadly, the arguing and fighting started once more and your mum became depressed and was admitted to hospital again. Dennis looked after both of you while she was having treatment, with help from a family support worker called Claire. She came in to help your dad and she made sure that you and Jordon had some breakfast and that you went to nursery during the day.

When your mum came home things didn't really improve and one day, when you were just 2 years old, Dennis said that he didn't feel that he could live with your mum any longer and he left the flat. Your mum thinks that he went back to Birmingham but she is not sure and she says that she hasn't seen him since that day.

Your mum continued to look after you and Jordon with some help from Claire, the family support worker and from Fiona, the social worker. You still went to Happy Days Nursery during the week, but your mum's mental health was not good and she started doing some very odd things. The nursery assistants noticed that on some days your mum's behaviour was strange; for instance on some winter days, when it was cold, you came to nursery in summer clothes and in the summer, when it was warm, she dressed you in your winter clothes. One day it was very sunny and you arrived in your winter coat and hat and although you were so hot, she didn't want to take your coat off! It was such a hot day and the nursery assistants were so worried that you would overheat – and that is quite dangerous for young children – that once your mum had left they undressed you and put you in one of the spare summer dresses they kept at the nursery. Your mum was very cross with them when she picked you up at the end of the day, and after this she stopped taking you to nursery.

By now Jordon should have started school, but she wouldn't let him go. She kept you and Jordon in the flat and when Fiona heard that you were not at nursery and Jordon was not at school she was very worried about you, so she went to the flat to see you. All the windows in the flat were shut, your mum had drawn all the curtains and she didn't have any lights on. She didn't answer the door and Fiona thought that no one was in, but then she heard your mum's voice. Your mum wouldn't let her or anyone else into the flat to make sure that you were okay. This was all to do with your mum's mental illness and her mind becoming all muddled up again. It was another emergency!

This time Fiona decided that she would definitely need to go to court to ask the judge for an Emergency Order so that she could make sure that you and Jordon were safe. Once she had this she was able to go back to the flat with Claire and with the police and they had to break in. You and Jordon were both frightened and very upset, but when you saw that Claire was there you both stopped crying and she cuddled you while the police and Fiona talked to your mum about you going to a foster home.

So this is why, when you were 4 years old and Jordon was 5 years old, you both went to stay with Julie, the foster carer who had looked after Jordon when he was a baby. Julie lived in a small flat and she didn't have much room there. She usually only looked after babies, and then only one at a time, but as it was an emergency and she remembered Jordon, she said that she would be able to look after both of you for a little while.

Here's Julie with both of you.

You stayed with Julie just for a week and then you moved to another foster carer, Kay. Kay had more space in her house. She had been a foster carer for a very long time and she often looked after children of your age, so this was a good place for you to stay. You and Jordon shared a bedroom and you liked this as you had always slept in the same bedroom at your mum's flat. You said that it made you feel safe knowing that your brother was there too.

Kay in her living room.

And here's Kay's house.

You both seemed to settle at Kay's home quite quickly, although at first the only thing you would eat was jam sandwiches; but gradually your appetite improved and soon you were eating all sorts of things. You loved being able to play in the garden. You had always lived in flats so hadn't had a garden before. At first you kept calling it the park. Kay was also a grandmother and you liked playing with her little grandchildren when they came to visit.

Meanwhile your mum went to hospital again and when she was feeling better she went back to her flat. Fiona had lots of discussions with your mum, and meetings with her and her social worker and with the doctors who knew your mum, especially with her psychiatrist. Psychiatrists are special doctors who understand a great deal about the brain and how it works, and they try to help people when their minds become ill.

The psychiatrist spent a long time talking to your mum and knew her quite well. She said that it was clear that your mum loved you and Jordon very much, but with the type of mental illness she has, she might never get completely better. She said that there will probably be many times when she does strange things again and then she will need to be looked after in hospital again. This would mean that you and Jordon would spend your time coming in and out of foster care and you might have to go to different foster homes each time and this would not be good for you.

Everyone at those meetings agreed that Tania loved you and Jordon very much, and when she was well she was able to look after you, but when she was ill, and that happened so many times, her behaviour was strange and sometimes quite scary. At these times your mum wasn't able to do all the things that parents must do to keep children safe and to help you to grow into strong healthy adults.

Fiona tried to find your dad, to see if he could help, but no one knew where he was living and he could not be found. Fiona soon went back to the court to update the judge. Judges are very clever people and they have to make very important decisions about children and their futures. He listened to Fiona and asked if there was anyone else in the family who could help. The judge also asked her to try again to find your dad and suggested she should make some more enquires about any other family members. Before making a final decision he also said that he wanted another report from a psychiatrist, so that he could understand more about your mum and her illness.

So this is what happened and it took quite a long time. Fiona still couldn't find your dad, but she did go to see your mum's Aunty Maria. Aunty Maria said that she had so many things going on in her life and she was getting too old to look after young children. She was sorry that she couldn't help and she didn't know of any other relatives who would be able to look after you.

Eventually Fiona went back to court. This time the judge read all of the reports, including the one written by the psychiatrist, and he listened to everyone involved, including your mum. The judge agreed that although your mum loved you, because of her illness she wouldn't be able to look after you in the way you needed to be cared for and in the way you deserve. He also thought that at times you mum's behaviour would be very frightening for you to see.

Fiona told that judge that you and Jordon are such lovely children and that you needed to live in a home where you could both grow up together, somewhere that you could stay until you were adults. She also said that she knew that you love your mum very much and would want to see her sometimes and to know that she was okay.

You and Jordon said that you liked living with Kay and wished you could just stay with her and she had explained that you would be able to stay with her until Fiona found the right long-term foster home. Fiona also told the judge that you both said that you have a mum and didn't want another mum, so you didn't want to be adopted.

The judge listened to all of this and he agreed that you should stay in care and he granted a Care Order. This Order meant that Fiona could now make some very important decisions about you and could make plans for your future. She wanted you to have the best possible care.

Fiona came to see you and Jordon after court, and told you about the Care Order and the plans she was making to find you just the right foster family — a family where you could stay until you are grown up — a permanent foster family. Kay had always reminded you that she would be looking after you until the right foster family was found.

It took a bit of time — but that's exactly what happened.

8. Moving to Sharon and Pete's

Everyone agreed that Sharon and Pete were just the right foster family for you and Jordon. They knew what to do to help you grow into healthy, strong children.

Here are Sharon and Pete.

Sharon was born in Croydon and she has plenty of relatives and friends in the area. Pete is from Jamaica, like your mum, and he had come over to live in Croydon with his mum and dad when he was about 6 years old. Sharon and Pete met at school, they married when they were both 22 years old and they have two teenage sons.

They just knew that like other children, you would need lots of love and cuddles, plenty of sleep, good food, a warm house, clean clothes, lots of fun and playtimes, and just the right number of rules to make sure that you are kept safe and secure. Sharon and Pete had already had to give the social worker masses of information about themselves and all sorts of checks had been carried out.

The social worker had written a long report all about them, and they had all had to attend a Fostering Panel, where they had to answer loads of questions, before they were allowed to become foster carers.

They told the people on the panel that they didn't want to look after children just for a short while, as they wanted children to stay with them until they were grown up, so when they heard all about you they really hoped that you would be able to become part of their family. They had lots of discussions and attended many meetings and went to another panel, where they were asked lots of questions by people there, including a doctor, some social workers and other foster carers. This panel agreed that Sharon and Pete seemed just right and they would be able to look after you and your brother, so the panel agreed that they should be your permanent foster carers

Sharon and Pete met you after this meeting in 2014, at your foster home. You were 6 years old, almost 7.

You and Jordon meeting Sharon and Pete.

You remember something of this first meeting, and said that you felt very nervous and you were very shy at first and stayed by Kay's side, but you relaxed as you got to know them. Sharon said that she really liked your purple jumper and she told you that purple was one of her favourite colours, and you were pleased about that and you took her to your bedroom to show her some of your other favourite clothes. You were soon showing them your chatty, bubbly personality.

Here you are again at that first meeting – perhaps you were all feeling a little nervous.

Sharon and Pete also told you that they were going to be meeting your mum, in a few days time. They were looking forward to this, so you were pleased about this too.

Sharon and Pete meeting Tania.

Over the next few weeks you got to know Sharon and Pete, and they got to know all about you too. They came to the foster home nearly every day and they showed you photographs of the family and the house. You still had some worries about moving, but you were pleased to know that Kay had told them all about you and they knew that you don't like broccoli or cauliflower and that you and Jordon like to leave your bedroom door open at night and that Kay leaves a night-light on the landing, and that sometimes you need to go to the toilet at night. Sharon told you that she didn't like broccoli and cauliflower very much either, and she said that she would buy a night-light for the landing before you moved in.

Kay took you and Jordon to visit your new home so that you could see were you would be living and where you would sleep. You also met your foster brothers, and again you were quite shy at first, but when they told you that one of their favourite programmes was Doctor Who, you had plenty to talk about. You were also able to visit your new school and you met your new teacher.

A few weeks later, just after your 7th birthday, Kay packed up all of your toys, books and clothes. She also gave you your memory box, full of the special things you had put in it, and she gave you an album full of photographs and lovely memories of the time you had lived with her. There are more photographs of your mum and dad in there too. Kay said that she would stay in touch with you and that when you had settled in to your new home she would love to come to visit you.

And then you and Jordon made the journey to your new home in Croydon with Sharon and Pete and that was how you became part of your foster family.

Of course it was all a bit strange at first. You had to get used to the new house and family, and everything was a bit different and there were different house rules and routines to get used to.

Jordon seemed to settle quickly and he liked having 2 big brothers, but it took a little longer for you and you missed Kay at first.

Gradually you settled in and you began to feel more comfortable and you liked your little bedroom, although at first you missed sharing a room with Jordon. You said the room felt more like yours once you had put some of your posters on the wall and some of your favourite cuddly toys on the bed. You also liked your new school and quickly made some new friends there.

Of course, you still miss your mum and you look forward to seeing her. As long as she is well enough, you see her at the family centre during the school holidays. Usually Sharon and Jordon go with you and the social worker is there with your mum to make sure that she is okay.

Here you are with your mum.

Kay has also been to see you and that was nice too.

9. More about Tandi

Here you are with your foster family.

You have been living with Sharon and Pete for quite a long time now and they have continued to care for you and they have both said that they love having you as part of their family. I think that you like living with Sharon and Pete too, and you have grown especially close to Sharon. Sometimes the two of you will leave all of the boys at home with Pete and you will have a day out shopping together and treat yourselves to a pizza for lunch!

You have fun with Pete too and he is the one who takes you and the boys to the skate park.

And there have been lots of fun times. There have been family days out and you have had your 8th birthday and you will soon be celebrating your 9th birthday.

You have had your first Christmas with them and Sharon and Pete came to your sports day at school and to hear you singing in the school concert.

Of course Sharon and Pete still remember all of the important things that Kay told them about you and they now know lots of other things too. For instance they know that your:

Favourite TV programme is Dr Who and you also like Hannah Montana

Favourite food is pizza or pasta

Favourite game is Twister

Favourite animal is a dog

Favourite drink is hot chocolate

Favourite colour is purple

Favourite film is Minions.

So, as you can see, they know so much about you. They also know that like all children, sometimes you feel happy and sometimes you feel sad. They also know that sometimes you like to look in your memory box and at the photograph album that your foster carer gave you and sometimes you think about Kay and about your mum and you wonder what happened to your dad and where he is now.

Sharon also knows that sometimes, when you are thinking about all of these things, you feel quite sad and become very quiet, but you don't tell anyone. I wonder if you are a bit like the 'Nifflenoo called Nevermind' and, just like him, you tuck all of those feelings away deep inside – I wonder if you agree!

I just wonder, as I know Sharon and Pete understand all of these feelings, and they hope that you know that they will always be there to listen to you and to give you a cuddle when you need one.

Sharon and Pete also know that you have lots of plans and hopes for the future. You think that you might join a gymnastics club and perhaps one day train for the Olympics, but you are not sure. You are certainly very sporty and talented and you would be very good at this, although I wonder if you will agree!

And you never know, perhaps one day when your teacher says Tandi, you are doing very well, or when Sharon says that you have brains and beauty, or when Pete says that you are a really good athlete, or when one of your friends says that you have nice hair, or when someone says that you have a very bright future ahead of you, then you might just say:

Yes, I agree!

10. 2017 and Onwards

Now this may seem like the end of this book, but your life adventure will continue and there will be lots more fun and happy times to come!

[You could scan some more photographs of recent family celebrations, outings, holidays etc. to finish the book, and Tandi and her foster carers could carry on adding some photographs and comments each year to continue the book.]

CHAPTER 8

Final Thoughts

There is clearly a moral and a legal duty to gather photographs and record as much information as possible about members of the birth family and other significant adults in the child's history for all children in care. The Adoption and Children Act 2002 highlighted the need for children to be given comprehensive information about themselves, and further guidance, specifically in relation to the provision of life story books, has been set out in subsequent Statutory Guidance on Adoption (Department for Education 2013), and National Minimum Standards (Department for Education 2014, Standard 2). A clear account of the family history and the circumstances which led to a child coming into care is vital for all children.

Whilst this new format for the child's life story book – present → past → present → future – is not suitable for all children in care, for children for whom permanency is the plan, this is likely to be the most appropriate model. The book should not be finalized until some time after the permanent placement, when the child has had time to settle, or within 10 days of the adoption celebratory hearing.

This approach will call for 'inter-team' and, in some instances, inter-agency co-operation and commitment. Someone will need to take responsibility for co-ordinating and finishing the book. Responsibility may remain with the child's key worker or it may be more appropriate for the book to be completed by the permanency or adoption worker. But the very important 'middle' section, with information about the birth, the birth parents, the circumstances leading to the child coming into care and previous fostering placements, should be completed by the child's social worker and should be available pre-placement or shortly afterward. This also complies with current guidance specifying that the book should be given to the adopters in stages: 'The first stage is at the second statutory review of the child's placement with the prospective adopter' (Department for Education 2013, p.107). This will be the 'past' section and rest of the book can be completed over the following months and finalized after the celebratory hearing.

The social workers, ex-foster carers, current carers, adopters and birth family will each have a different, but equally valuable, perspective on the child's life. They each hold some memories and knowledge of the child's history and present circumstances. These different elements must be presented in a coherent way, so that the child's sense of self becomes more positive and integrated, and their understanding of their own history becomes less fragmented.

The book is about the child's life and it is written for the child, so it should provide a simple, honest, coherent narrative. It is just the first 'tier' and, although this alone will not ensure that a child has a clear understanding of their history, it is a good starting point. The book is just a basic tool for carers and adopters to build on, at the child's pace.

There are lessons to be learnt from our knowledge and work with care leavers and with adopted adults and the 'closed' adoptions of the past. Their 'need to know' and to find the 'missing pieces of the jigsaw' are well documented, but there is now a danger of overcompensating for the lack of information previously shared with children in care, and for those past secretive adoptions, and overwhelming today's children with too much detail too soon.

The life story book needs to be child friendly and, whilst acknowledging the difficulties, sadness and losses experienced, it should also be a celebration of the child's life. The book should leave the child with a positive sense of who they are and with hope for the future – not weighed down and overburdened by the birth parents' troubled history.

The work and expertise involved in compiling life story books and in collating the various sections should not be underestimated. Some agencies recognize this and now have dedicated staff (and a few have teams who specialize in this work) and the books they produce are of a high standard. However, there is a lack of consistency and there are far too many examples of poor practice, as the Coram/Bristol University research project highlights. While some adopters felt that 'using a life story book with their adopted children has been extremely positive', others felt that they were 'unusable...damaging and unhelpful' (Coram/Bristol University 2015, p.17).

If time and effort is put into creating a sensitive, child friendly life story book that can be used with confidence by carers and adoptive parents, then the book will achieve its purpose – and the workers involved will have made an important contribution to improving placement stability and helping the child move towards the positive future that he or she certainly deserves.

Information from Permanent Carers or Adoptive Parents for the Child's Life Story Book

Child's full name:

DOB:

Date child came to live with you:

Names of all immediate family members, including pets:

For carers, first name only of any other foster children living with you:

Does the child have a nickname and what does she/he call you, e.g. Mummy, Dad, Papa, Auntie, Nan, first name?

Names of any significant members of the extended family, e.g. aunts, grandparents, cousins and names child uses for them, e.g. Gran, Granny, Nana.

Where do they live and how often do you have contact with them?

How would you describe your child physically (colour of hair, eyes, build, etc.) and temperamentally?

Are there any developmental delays or health concerns?

What does your child like doing?

Does she/he have any particular hobbies, interests or collections?

What are your child's favourites, e.g. colour, food, drink, clothes, toys, games, TV programme, film, book, football team?

Describe your house or flat and surrounding area:

Is it in a town or in the country?

Do you have a garden or play area?

Are there any parks, schools, leisure facilities, shops, etc. nearby?

Does your child have her/his own bedroom or is it shared?

How is it decorated?

Is there a specific bedtime routine?

Does your child have a comforter or special cuddly toy?

Do you have any particular family rituals, e.g. meal times, 'take away' or film night, attending church, chapel, mosque?

Are religious festivals or specific days celebrated, e.g. Birthdays, Christmas, Easter, Diwali, Ramadan, Passover, Adoption or Placement Day, and if so how?

Name of playgroup/nursery/school attended. Is this within walking distance and if not how does she/he travel there?

When did your child start attending?

Names of teachers and of any particular friends:

Any positive or 'funny' comments staff have made or in school reports?

Your child's attitude to playgroup/nursery/school and favourite activities and subjects:

What does she/he like and dislike about playgroup/nursery/school?

Does she/he know any other children or adults who were or are in care or adopted? Is there anyone else in your immediate or extended family?

What do you think your child currently understands of the early history and the circumstances leading to her/him coming into care?

Do you have any details of the birth, e.g. name of hospital, weight, length, time?

When and where did you meet your child and what are your memories of that first meeting?

How was the introductory period organized and over what period of time?

What did/does your child call his/her ex-foster carers?

Were there other placements?

Do you have any photographs of previous carers and does your child have any particular memories of this time?

Are you and your child still in touch with them?

Did the ex-foster carers provide a memory box, book or photograph album?

Do you have photographs of birth relatives and are there any significant items from them in the memory box? If so, is your child aware of these?

Did you have any particular memories of the early weeks and months as a family?

How did/does your child show worries or anxiety, e.g. sleep disturbance, eating difficulties, enuresis, soiling, withdrawing, becoming hyperactive?

Do you have family holidays and if so where do you usually go?

Are there any holidays planned?

Does your child have any particular plans and aspirations for the future, e.g. learning to swim, to ride a bike, to play an instrument, becoming a hairdresser, a footballer or an astronaut, going to Disneyland?

Is there any contact with birth parents, siblings or other members of the birth family, and if so what are the arrangements? How does your child react to this contact?

If applicable, details of Special Guardianship or Adoption Order and of Celebration Hearing. For the latter, name of court, date and was it a male or female judge?

Did the judge make any particular or amusing comments, allow your child to sit on the judge's chair, try on the wig and give a certificate or other memento to your child?

What was the weather like, who else attended and how did you celebrate the day?

If your child's first name was changed or a new middle name was added, what is the significance of these names?

Is there other information you would like to include in your child's life story book?

Photographs will be scanned into the book and if you have any digital photographs please email them. It would be helpful to have a few photographs of the child when she/he was younger and as a baby if you have them, of your first meeting, the introductory period and the early days of the placement. If applicable, include photographs of your meeting with the birth family, with ex-foster carers, and of any recent ongoing contact with them or with the birth family.

The book should also have recent photographs of your child on her/his own, as well as a selection with you, with the nuclear family, and with other significant members of your extended family. Include photographs of your home and of child's bedroom. Please also include photographs of birthdays, family gatherings, celebrations (including the Adoption Celebratory Day), holidays, family days out, fun activities, nursery or school events and enjoying time with family and friends. These will all help your child feel that she/he is valued, loved, claimed by you and that she/he belongs to your family.

Information from Previous Foster Carers for the Child's Life Story Book

Child's name:

DOB:

Date child placed with you and date placement ended:

Names of all foster family members, including pets:

What did the child call you and what did you call him/her? Was there a nickname?

Did he/she come to you from the birth family or from another foster home?

Did you have any other foster children at that time? If so what were their first names? How did they get on and when did they leave?

If the child was previously with foster carers, what were the reasons for the move and did this happen in a planned way?

Did you meet the child before he/she was placed with you or was it an emergency placement?

What are your memories of the first meeting?

Did the child talk about his/her previous foster carers or have further contact with them? Did he/she have any photographs of the time spent with them?

Any particular memories of the first few days or weeks that he/she was with you?

How would you describe this child while he/she was living with you physically (colour of hair, eyes, build, etc.) and temperamentally.?

Did he/she have any health issues during this time?

What did the child like doing and did he/she have any particular hobbies/interests/collections?

Were you living in a house or flat and where was this?

Did he/she have their own bedroom or, if shared, who did he/she share with?

What were his/her favourites, e.g. colour, food, drink, clothes, toys, games, TV programme, film, book, football team or any other favourite things?

Were there any particular family rituals and celebrations? e.g. meal times, attending church or mosque or celebrations of birthdays or religious festivals?

Was there a regular bedtime routine? Did he/she have a comforter or favourite cuddly toy?

Did he/she sleep and eat well?

Names of any playgroup, nursery or schools attended:

When did he/she start playgroup/nursery/school and what year was the child in?

Any positive or 'funny' comments staff made:

Attitude to playschool/nursery/school:

Favourite subjects or activities and names of any significant teachers or friends:

What did he/she like and dislike about playgroup, nursery or school?

Were any significant milestones reached or achievements attained while the child was living with you, e.g. cut first tooth, learned to walk, to swim, to ride a scooter, joined beavers, brownies or dance class, first day at school, birthdays, holidays?

Any illnesses, accidents or operations?

Do you think he/she had any understanding of his/her early history and the circumstances leading to being fostered?

Did he/she talk about his/her birth family or ask questions? Was any life work done to help him/her with this?

Did he/she have much understanding of future plans and of the proposed move? Was any life work completed with the child to prepare for the transition?

Did you meet any members of the birth family? If so, how would you describe them and what are your memories of them?

Was there direct contact with his/her birth family? If so with whom, how often and where did this take place?

What was child's reaction to this contact?

Were you given any details about the child's birth?

Do you know who chose the child's names and if the names have a particular significance?

How did he/she show worries or anxiety, e.g. any sleep disturbance, eating difficulties, enuresis or soiling?

Do you have any fond or funny memories or anecdotes involving this child to include in the life story book?

Does the child have a memory box or book or photograph album of the time he/she spent with you?

Is there any other information you would like to share and to mention in the child's book?

Do you have any photographs of the child taken during the time he/she lived with you, and some photographs of you and your family to include in the life story book?

Information from Birth Parents for the Child's Life Story Book

(These 'prompts' will not be appropriate for all birth parents. Discretion and sensitivity will be needed and it is important to stress that this information is for the child's book. Some of the suggested questions could also be adapted to gather information for other birth family members.)

Child's name:

Name, DOB and relationship to child:

Information about you

How would you describe yourself physically, e.g. height, build, skin tone, colour of eyes and hair?

What hairstyles do you like and is your hair naturally straight, wavy or curly?

Do you like to change the colour of your hair and is it usually long, short or do you like to shave it all off?

What size shoes do your wear and what size are your clothes?

What type of clothes do you like to wear? Casual, sporty, smart?

Do you wear spectacles and if so do you know if you are short- or long-sighted?

How would you describe your personality, e.g. quiet, chatty, bubbly, outgoing, confident, shy, withdrawn, friendly, loud, calm, fiery?

How is your health and do you or any other members of your family have any health concerns or illnesses?

Do you have any particular hobbies or interests?

What sorts of things do you like doing?

Do you have a favourite colour, food, TV programme, football team or any other favourite things?

Where did you go to school?

What did you like about school and what did you dislike?

Did you have any favourite subjects?

Did you get a job when you left school/college and if so what did you do?

Have you had other jobs and are you working now?

Are you living on your own, with a partner, with your children or with other family members?

Do you have other children and if so what are their names and ages?

Where do they live?

Is there any other information about yourself that you would like to share or to include in your child's book?

Do you also have any recent photographs of yourself and photographs of when you were younger that could be copied for your child and scanned into the life story book?

Information about your child

Where and when was he/she born?

How was the birth and were there any complications?

Did he/she arrive on time or was he/she early or late?

What did he/she look like and did he/she have any hair?

Did the baby need any special care in the first few days/weeks?

Did any family members or friends visit the baby in hospital?

When was he/she discharged?

Was he/she discharged with you to your home?

If so, where was this and who else was there at that time?

Who registered his/her birth and who chose the names?

Do these names have any particular significance?

What was your child like as a baby/toddler/young child and how would you describe him/her?

Did he/she have any health issues during this time?

Can you remember any funny things he/she said or did during those early years?

Is there any other information or memories that you would like to share?

Do you have any baby or early photographs of your child that we can copy and give to him/her and scan into the life story book?

References

Bowlby, J. (1992) *A Secure Base: Clinical Applications of Attachment Theory.* London: Routledge.

Bowlby, J. (2007) *The Making and Breaking of Affectional Bonds.* London: Routledge.

Burnell, A. and Vaughan, J. (2008) 'Remembering Never to Forget and Forgetting Never to Remember: Re-thinking Life Story Work.' In B. Luckock and M. Lefevre (eds) *Direct Work: Social Work with Children and Young People in Care.* London: CoramBAAF.

Coram/ Bristol University (2015) 'Adopters' views on their children's life story books.' *Adoption and Fostering Journal 39,* 119–134.

Department for Education (2013) *Statutory Guidance on Adoption.* London: Department for Education.

Department for Education (2014) *Adoption: National Minimum Standards.* London: Department for Education.

Fahlberg, V. (2003) *A Child's Journey through Placement.* London: CoramBAAF.

Fursland, E. (2013) *Facing Up to Facebook: A Survival Guide for Adoptive Families.* London: Coram/BAAF.

Gliori, D. (1999) *No Matter What.* London: Bloomsbury Children's Books.

Hammond, S. and Cooper, N. (2013) *Digital Life Story Work. Using Technology to Help Young People Make Sense of their Experiences.* London: CoramBAAF.

Harwin, J., Alrouh, B., Palmer, M., Broadhurst, K. and Swift, S. (2016) 'A national study of the usage of supervision orders and special guardianship orders over time. Briefing paper no 1: Special guardianship orders.' Brunel and Lancaster University. Available from: www.nuffieldfoundation.org

O'Malley, B. (2004) *Lifebooks: Creating A Treasure for The Adopted Child.* Winthrop, MA: Adoptions-Works.

Rose, R. and Philpot, T. (2005) *The Child's Own Story: Life Story Work with Traumatized Children.* London: Jessica Kingsley Publishers.

Ryan, T. and Walker, R. (2016) *Life Story Work.* London: CoramBAAF.

Selwyn, J., Wijedasa, D. and Meakings, S. (2014) 'Beyond the Adoption Order: challenges, interventions and adoption disruption.' Research Report. London: Department for Education.

Sunderland, M. (2001) *A Nifflenoo Called Nevermind.* London: Speechmark Publishing Ltd.

van Gulden, H. and Riedel, C. (1998–1999) *In Search of Self: Reclaiming and Healing the Lost, Wounded and Missing Parts of Self.* Minneapolis, MN: Adoptive Family Counseling Center.

Verrier, N. (2009) *The Primal Wound: Understanding the Adopted Child.* London: CoramBAAF.

Wrench, K. and Naylor, L. (2013) *Life Story Work with Children Who are Fostered or Adopted: Creative Ideas and Activities.* London: Jessica Kingsley Publishers.

Further Reading

Archer, C. (1999) *First Steps in Parenting the Child Who Hurts: Tiddlers and Toddlers.* London: Jessica Kingsley Publishers.

Archer, C. (1999) *Next Steps in Parenting the Child Who Hurts: Tykes and Teens.* London: Jessica Kingsley Publishers.

Archer, C. and Burnell, A. (2003) *Trauma Attachment and Family Permanence.* London: Jessica Kingsley Publishers.

Archer, C. and Gordon, C. (2006) *New Families, Old Scripts: A Guide to the Language of Trauma and Attachment in Adoptive Families.* London: Jessica Kingsley Publishers.

Bowlby, J. (1992) *A Secure Base: Clinical Applications of Attachment Theory.* London: Routledge.

Bowlby, J. (2007) *The Making and Breaking of Affectional Bonds.* London: Routledge.

Fahlberg, V. (2003) *A Child's Journey through Placement.* London: BAAF.

Foster, C. (2008) *Big Steps for Little People: Parenting Your Adopted Child.* London: Jessica Kingsley Publishers.

Grinder, M. (2007) *The Elusive Obvious: The Science of Non-verbal Communication.* Battle Ground, WA: Michael Grinder & Associates.

Hughes, D. (2004) *Building the Bonds of Attachment: Awakening Love in Deeply Troubled Children.* Lanham, MD: Rowman & Littlefield.

Hughes, D. (2007) *Attachment-Focused Family Therapy.* New York: W.W. Norton & Company.

Lacher, D. Nichols, T. and May, J. (2005) *Connecting with Kids through Stories: Using Narratives to Facilitate Attachment in Adopted Children.* London: Jessica Kingsley Publishers.

Luckock, B. and Lefevre, M. (2008) *Direct Work: Social Work with Children and Young People in Care.* London: BAAF.

MacLeod, J. and Macrae, S. (2006) *Adoption Parenting: Creating a Toolbox, Building Connections.* Warren, NJ: EMK Press.

O'Malley, B. (2004) *Lifebooks: Creating a Treasure for the Adopted Child.* Winthrop, MA: Adoptions-Works.

Romaine, M., Turley, T. and Tuckey, N. (2007) *Preparing Children for Permanence.* London: BAAF.

Rose, R. and Philpot, T. (2005) *The Child's Own Story: Life Story Work with Traumatized Children.* London: Jessica Kingsley Publishers.

Rosen, S. (1991) *My Voice Will Go With You: The Teaching Tales of Milton H. Erickson.* London: Norton.

Ryan, T. and Walker, R. (2016) *Life Story Work.* London: CoramBAAF.

van Gulden, H. and Reidel, C. (1998–1999) *In Search of Self: Reclaiming and Healing the Lost, Wounded and Missing Parts of Self.* Minneapolis, MN: Adoptive Family Counseling Center.

van Gulden, H. and Vick, C. (2010) *Learning the Dance of Attachment: An Adoptive Foster Parent's Guide to Nurturing Healthy Developments.* Minneapolis, MN: Adoptive Family Counseling Center.